# CRAIG REVEL HORWOOD

# CRAIG REVEL HORWOOD

## *Tales* FROM THE *Dance Floor*

Michael O'Mara Books

First published in Great Britain in 2013 by
Michael O'Mara Books Limited
9 Lion Yard
Tremadoc Road
London SW4 7NQ

A CIP catalogue record for this book is available from the British Library.

Papers used by Michael O'Mara Books Limited are natural, recyclable
products made from wood grown in sustainable forests. The manufacturing
processes conform to the environmental regulations of the country of origin.

ISBN: 978-1-78243-151-0 in hardback print format
ISBN: 978-1-78243-161-9 in ebook format

1 2 3 4 5 6 7 8 9 10

Designed and typeset by Ana Bježančević
Printed and bound by CPI Group (UK) Ltd, Croydon, CR0 4YY
www.mombooks.com

# CONTENTS

# PROLOGUE

Four years ago, when I sat down to write my autobiography, *All Balls and Glitter*, I poured my heart out on the page and found it a liberating experience. It was the first time I had put down on paper the whole truth about the colourful and sometimes painful past that had shaped me and made me the man I am today, and it felt good to lay it all bare. What I wasn't expecting was the reaction. I was suddenly front-page news – for all the wrong reasons. But as Oscar Wilde famously said, 'The only thing worse than being talked about is *not* being talked about.'

On the other hand, I had many people approaching me in the street and telling me how much they had enjoyed reading the book, which was fabulous, and it was great that

*Strictly Come Dancing* fans got to see the real person behind TV's 'Mr Nasty'.

Much has happened since then. I have become a full British citizen, passed a driving test, rubbed shoulders with royalty and been in and out of love. Through my *Strictly* notoriety, I have found myself in the most bizarre situations – answering quiz questions on the scariest rollercoaster in America, eating bull's testicles disguised as fruit and being parachuted into Wembley. But perhaps the oddest moment in recent years is when I found myself doing a nightly Charleston with a well-known former Cabinet Minister.

In 2010, I was asked to take over the *Strictly Come Dancing Live* tour, which Arlene Phillips had directed for the first two years. I had already directed the opening of the Commonwealth Games in Manchester, in 2002, as well as staging several operas in big arenas, so I was used to putting on productions on a grand scale. The bigger the better, I say – bring it on.

Moira Ross, the then producer of *Strictly*, was overseeing the live show on behalf of the BBC and one day we held a meeting with the execs and creative people from the production company, Phil McIntyre Entertainments, and the BBC. The room was full of people and everyone was chatting away noisily – until I walked in. Suddenly there was stony silence. You could have heard a pin drop. After a long pause, Moira piped up.

'Craig,' she said, in her most coercive voice. 'We were just thinking … how would you feel about dancing with Ann Widdecombe?'

My immediate feeling was horror. 'I'm a judge, darling,' I said. 'I sit behind a desk and judge the dances. The viewers don't even know I have legs!'

Of course, after a moment's reflection, I said yes. I thought it was a crazy idea but could be really good fun and the audience would love it. Even so, it nearly killed me.

Our initial thought was to have Ann flying down from the rafters – as she had in her tango with Anton du Beke on the TV show – and having me flying out of the judges' desk to meet her, mid-air. But the rigs proved too expensive for the live show so we devised a dance based on their *Titanic* routine. Ann began by calling out Anton's name as she searched in vain, before bumping into her arch nemesis, Craig Revel Horwood, in the fog. I took the opportunity to have a bit of fun with it, and to have a dig at myself in the choreography. I made it a Charleston, because I have done a lot of shows set in the 1920s and '30s, so the flapper thing appealed to me, plus it meant there was a lot of side-by-side steps. But we included every one of Anton's lifts from the show and, although Ann had lost two stone, she still weighed ten and a half stone – and it's all dead weight. I could lift a twelve-stone dancer quite easily but because Ann is not trained, and not capable of holding the right positions, it is incredibly difficult to lift her.

On the first day of rehearsals, I was quite apprehensive because I've never danced with a celebrity contestant before on *Strictly* and my reputation was at stake. As a judge, and the harshest judge on the panel, I was not thrilled by the prospect of the tables being turned.

On top of my nerves about the performance, I was quite nervous of Ann herself. She's quite scary. I'd met her on set, but not socially or anything, and she seemed a bit frightening. Anton du Beke, who partnered her on *Strictly*, told me a little bit about what it was like to work with her.

The lovely Anton gave me advice on dancing with Ann, whom he had partnered in the show.

'She can't hear music, she can't count in time,' he said. 'She is completely rhythmically challenged.' In fact, Ann would be the first to admit to that. But I convinced myself that it couldn't be *that* bad … it might even be a bit of a doddle, because I thought, 'I'll do a bit of dancing around her and we'll do a few steps together.' I put together the simplest steps I possibly could and, armed with my Charleston routine, turned up in plenty of time at the rehearsal studio.

After a preliminary chat, we launched into the steps – and I began to see the challenge ahead of me. I'd say, 'Ann, we're going off on the left leg,' and I'd step on her heel because she'd gone off on the right leg. But not consistently. This changed every minute, so I was never quite sure what foot she was going to step off on, and that, when you're trying to do unison work, is a nightmare. And Anton was certainly speaking the truth when he said she can't hear the music, because she really can't. We were dancing to 'Let's Do It', the Cole Porter classic, so, after umpteen times of me saying, 'Listen to the music!' I changed tack.

'If you can't hear the beat, go on the lyrics,' I said. 'When they say, "Birds do it, bees do it", you do this step.' But she still couldn't get it so the first rehearsal was a car crash.

To make matters worse, because I hadn't danced for years and I was quite unfit, I was carrying a lot of weight, so after five minutes of Charleston, I said 'Oh, darling, I'm exhausted.' I had to sit down – I was more exhausted than she was. After a nightmare start, I thought, 'What have I let myself in for? Am I going to be able to do this for eight shows a week?'

It got to the point where we had done it so many times in the rehearsal room that we finally had it … and the next day, when we came to rehearse again, it had all gone out the window. She couldn't remember any of the routines so, eventually, we decided that I would shout what's coming up next, or I'd give her a great, big, enormous nod when she had to go down on the floor. It turned out Anton had been shouting over the music all through the series of *Strictly*, smiling through gritted teeth, and saying, 'Ann, get up now. This is the next section.' I had to do the same. My microphone was switched off for the dance so all the way through the routine, during the live tour performances, I was saying, 'Now this is where we come together. This is the aeroplane bit.' I had to use simple terminology so she would know what I was talking about. Then I'd hiss, 'Now we're going to step on the left and kick the right leg.' And she would step on the right and kicked the left!

I have a wonderful photo on the wall at home that shows Ann in one lift where she's in a star shape and I've got to put my hand right next to her crotch, and the other one just underneath her boobs. I had to get underneath her sizeable bust to get into her rib cage with my left hand, then my right hand had to go inside her inside thigh and then I'd lift her so she was like a star fish being twirled around. Amazingly, considering her famously Victorian values and her resistance to any 'sexy' moves on *Strictly*, she went completely along with it. But dancers get into all sorts of intimate positions, and it has to be done.

The audience absolutely loved our dance. It brought the house down, every time. The press loved it and everywhere we went, there was a huge buzz in the audience about it. But the whole thing nearly put me in traction for months! Of course, to add insult to my considerable injury, my fellow judges, Len and Bruno, scored it pretty harshly. I think the highest mark we got was a two.

Ann was a great sport on tour and we became good friends. We make an odd couple, because you wouldn't expect a Tory politician and a camp old hoofer like me to get on – we both come from very different backgrounds in life, and have done very different things. But when she had to rely on me for the lifts, and trust me not to drop her, or hurt her, all that is broken down. Little did we know that that Charleston was the beginning of a double act that would go on for a few years more.

CHAPTER 1

# THE SHOW MUST GO ON

I n June 2009, as I sat watching ducks on the little river outside the Watermill Theatre in Newbury, I got a call from Arlene Phillips. In the previous weeks, I had been completely absorbed with my production of *Spend Spend Spend*, which was about to open at the Watermill, and at that moment, I had come out to answer emails and messages on my regular seat in the theatre car park, which was the only place I could get any reception.

Arlene's voice, on the other end of the line, was distraught.

'I'm not doing *Strictly* this year,' she cried.

'What?' I replied, shocked.

'I'm not on the panel this year.' I couldn't believe what I was hearing.

'Well, why not?' I asked, 'What's happened?'

'I don't know,' she said. 'I can't really say. I was just told that I was no longer required on the show.

I was shocked because I thought she was an established part of the judging crew. It just hadn't occurred to me that the line-up of the judges – the Fearsome Foursome – would be subject to change. After six successful series, Arlene was a household name and her credentials were impeccable. Viewers knew about her big West End shows, including *We Will Rock You* and her success with dance troupe Hot Gossip, and they understand her background in choreography. I was surprised that Arlene was to be dropped.

We arranged to have dinner as soon as we could because I wanted the truth, I wanted to hear what Arlene had been told, but she didn't want to talk about it, she just wanted to come back. Then the news broke in the press and it was revealed she was being replaced with Alesha Dixon.

The backlash was incredible. The BBC was falsely accused of ageism for sacking an older woman in favour of a younger one, and that story ran for a year. Even Parliament got involved, with Harriet Harman, who was Deputy Labour Leader and the Minister for Equality at the time, making a speech about it in the House of Commons, and calling for Arlene's reinstatement. Everyone was jumping on the age-discrimination bandwagon for their own purposes. All except Arlene, who was keeping quiet about the whole thing because she was devastated.

At the same time, the whole storm wasn't easy for Alesha and she got a lot of flak, which I was happy to dampen down. Whatever had been decided, it wasn't Alesha's fault. She had just accepted an extremely attractive job offer, so I was quite happy to work in her defence, but it was a really tough time.

My fellow judges, Bruno Tonioli and Len Goodman, were in America working on *Dancing with the Stars*, so the publicity fell to me, and there was an enormous amount of pressure to give Alesha the qualification and validation the audience needed.

Being a notoriously opinionated judge, and being known for my honesty, I did not want to pull the wool over anyone's eyes or let my sense of honesty go, so I focussed on the positives. With every negative there's a positive and when I watch a dance routine I can see both, so I then have to choose what to say about that person that's going to help them on their journey through *Strictly*. It was the same with Alesha. Although she was being horribly judged by the press, by the audience and it seemed like she could do absolutely no right, I was saying, 'Give her a go.'

When I'm directing or choreographing, I implement cast changes all the time, because sometimes the dynamic changes, so I could sort of understand the need for change.

The BBC wanted someone that could represent the ethnic community but it would have been nice if there had been someone from the world of dance.

Additionally, Alesha was more 'street' than any of us, it was like 'Wazzup' and 'yo', which is a good thing if you want younger viewers. Unfortunately, the existing viewers didn't seem to like that because they were always questioning, 'What does she know about dance?'

But Alesha's main plus point was that she'd been through the show herself and trained for three months with a world champion – the wonderful Matt Cutler – so she was trained very, very well. She won the trophy in series five, so, in her defence, she was the only one on that panel of judges that had lived the *Strictly* experience from the beginning, from the first casting to the first dance lesson, all the way through to the annihilation by the judges, the criticism and the win. And the people voted, we didn't, so she was the people's choice.

I was shocked and horrified when there was so much negativity about her joining the judging panel. It's not easy, everyone thinks it's a really easy job – maybe we make it look easy – but we're attuned to it. I'm used to giving criticism because that's my job, as a director and a choreographer, and I get to cast the shows that I direct and choreograph, whereas in *Strictly* I don't, it's a *fait accompli*. I find out who is in each series an hour before the press and then I have to do all the research on them in that hour before the first phone calls start and journalists are asking, 'Craig, what do you think this one's going to be like?'

'Well just by looking at their head shot …' I reply. I have to form opinions pretty quick and it's not easy. So when the world is watching just you, because you're the replacement, there's a lot of pressure. She did thank me for my support and we had a chat about how she would face those first few weeks. I advised her just to speak her mind.

'If you think something's wrong, speak it,' I said. 'If you see something technical that you don't like, say so, because you can't keep talking about hair and make-up and costume for eternity. The reason why you're on this panel is to judge the dancing so it's good to throw in a bit of "When I was on *Strictly*, I was always told to straighten my legs in a Rumba", and that sort of thing.' After all, she had experience to talk about from that point of view.

Understandably, in the first week or two, she did go to pieces and she was heavily criticized. She had to try to work through that and she was pretty upset about what people were saying, not only on Twitter – because people can be foul on Twitter, and she was blocking hundreds of people a day – but also in the press. It was hard for her, and she got emotional, but Alesha's made of strong stuff and is really not afraid to speak her mind – and she's used to criticism. In the end, I think she got through it rather well.

Once the first year was over, it calmed down a little bit and people grew to like her, because she was being a little bit more of a comedian, she was being a little bit looser, she was becoming herself a little bit more.

The problem for Arlene, and potentially for all the judges, was that we only signed yearly contracts. If you're smart in this industry, or lucky, you get yourself a five-year deal, but we were just going from one year to the next and that had always been the case. When we were first gathered together, for the initial series in May 2004, nobody knew how long it would last. The producers told us, 'It might last three weeks, or full term, we don't know what the audience might think of it.'

Even after the first series, we weren't sure there would be a second. One day in August, I was walking down the main street in Bregenz, Austria, where I was choreographing a Kurt Weill operetta called *Der Kuhhandel*, for the Bregenz Festival, when someone from the BBC rang me.

'We're doing another series, to run up to Christmas,'

they said. 'Would you like to judge it?' I was really excited because, as it happened, I had a couple of things planned for the following year, but I didn't have anything lined up until Christmas, so it fitted in perfectly. So I signed for another series, and after that, yearly. That kept their options open but it also kept my options open if I didn't want to do it any more, for any reason.

As soon as we finished the final, every year, it was 'Bye bye', and never 'See you next year'. Last year, when Darcey Bussell came on board, was the first time that we'd actually been approached about the following year.

It's the same, and even more precarious, for the dancers. We lose professionals every year, because the celebrities are hired first and the dancers are only rehired if they are the right person to partner one of those celebrities. But they are never 'dropped', because the producers like to 'keep them in the *Strictly* family'. The reality and truth is that they are no longer in the competitive side of the show, but many come back to do bits and pieces.

For Arlene, it was a bitter blow and she still hasn't fully got over it. In fact, I think she would like to come back, but there's been so much water under the bridge now. If you don't feel wanted somewhere, the last thing you want to do is go back, but she misses it something terrible, and it's really sad.

The upside of the whole thing was the fact that she received an awful lot of attention, and that gave rise to opportunities that may never have been open to her. A year of publicity, of being on the front of the paper, is unquestionably, without a doubt, one of the most important things that's happened to her in her life. She was hired for *The One Show* and wrote newspaper columns, and last year she was honoured with a CBE.

The year after she was let go, the ITV National Television Awards invited her to choreograph a section and dance in it.

Later that summer, I joined celebrity guests, including Germaine Greer, Liz McClarnon of Atomic Kitten, Bill Paterson, *Cold Feet* star John Thomson and TV presenter Andi Oliver for a culinary experience like no other. We were invited on to *Heston's Feasts*, in which chef Heston Blumenthal recreates famous dishes from different periods of history. Ours was the medieval feast – and we had no idea what we had let ourselves in for when we arrived at the studio in Kentish Town.

I knew it was a medieval feast, obviously, and we were there to eat and comment on the food, but what I was about to receive made me truly incredulous.

We were given riddles and clues as to what was in all of

the dishes, although I never actually found out the whole truth until I watched a re-run of the programme some time later.

After hair and make-up we were seated in the green room and given a couple of drinks – no doubt designed to loosen our tongues. We were then ushered through into an opulent dining room, decorated in medieval splendour, and we sat down to a great, big, fabulous medieval feast. In the centre of the large table was our appetiser, which was a big bowl of fruit – or what appeared to be fruit – with quite a few plums on the top. I picked a nice fat juicy one and took a healthy bite. Oh my God, what a shock I got.

Instead of the sweet plum taste I was expecting, I got a mouthful of bulls' balls! It was filled with testicle pâté – bulls' plums if you like. That was Heston's joke. It just tasted like pâté, so it was actually quite nice, but it's odd when you're expecting a certain flavour, like fruit, and you get that instead, so that sent me reeling. But it was a very clever idea because each fruit had a different savoury filling, so we munched our way through those.

After that, we had this really nasty-looking lamprey starter. There was a big fish tank in the room and then they pulled out the fish, did a bit of chopping, then served up the lamprey with odd-looking sinewy stuff on the top – which turned out to be deep-fried nerve. The fish looked raw and the plate was covered in blood, but it wasn't real blood. Again, the whole thing was a trick. Heston and his talented chefs had put the uncooked fish head that they'd chopped off onto a cooked one, so they were no more offensive than sardines in the end, but because of the fake blood, and because it looked like fresh eel, it actually made me heave. And the deep-fried nerves were ghastly.

Germaine Greer was tasting everything and she started munching on the raw fish head, which was only there to convince us we were eating something that was medieval and horrific. Yuck! So that course wasn't a thrill, I must say.

The main course was four-and-twenty blackbirds baked in a pie, but as it's illegal to kill blackbirds in the UK, Heston used pigeons instead. The big double doors opened and they wheeled in this enormous dish, which must have measured at least two metres across, and then they lifted the top crust of pastry and all the pigeons flew out.

Everyone was screaming and one of the unleashed birds decided this was a good time to go to the toilet and dropped a large dollop of excrement on Andi's head! She had dreadlocks in, and it landed right on the top. Of course, rather than being sympathetic, we all collapsed into helpless laughter.

After our eventful introduction to the main course, they served proper little pots of pigeon pie, which were absolutely gorgeous. I was thoroughly enjoying myself.

Main course over, we were sent out of the room while they set up the dessert, and when we came back, and the table was beautifully laid, with knives and forks and spoons, candles and napkins. It all looked wonderful – except there was no pudding.

Then they said, 'Right, there's your dessert,' and we soon discovered that everything on the table was edible – *everything*. We ate the knives, the forks, the spoons, the napkins. Even the candles, which were alight when we came in, were edible. They tasted of chocolate and the napkins, which were icing sugar, looked exactly like real napkins. When I first walked in, I picked up the cutlery and thought it was quite light, but it had a funny texture, and then it started melting in my hand. Having discovered it was all edible, I bit directly into a candle and I was covered in a sweet white goo. But it was absolutely gorgeous. They were made of white chocolate with a filling of *crème anglaise* and they had a tube inside, containing some sort of paraffin, which is how they could have them burning when we came in. It was amazing – they looked so real.

As we ate, they brought in a pork pie, which seemed a weird choice in the middle of the dessert. But it was actually made from ice cream. There was no way you could tell by looking at it and it even had a little layer of aspic jelly between the 'crust' and the 'meat', so it looked incredible. It was absolute genius.

Although it was a half-hour show, it was a long day of filming. We were kept waiting an hour in between courses while they set everything up, and there was a whole gallery of people watching us on hidden cameras, so it was a very weird experience all round. It turned out to be an eight-hour dinner – and undoubtedly the most memorable meal of my life.

I haven't looked at a plum in the same way since.

Shortly after this unique experience I was packing my bags, once again, for my annual trip to New Zealand to judge *Dancing With the Stars*. Little did I know that this was to be the last time.

I really love New Zealand and New Zealanders. The country is awesome and the people are outgoing and friendly. The job also provided me with the luxury of seeing my family, as we only filmed on a Tuesday so I had the rest of the week off to travel and see the sights. Over the previous years I was able to take my mum and my eldest sister Sue on wonderful trips around the Marlborough Sounds and to all the amazing vineyards of that region.

The year before that we had stayed at The Bay of Many

Coves Resort in Marlborough. Mum had never been in a helicopter before so, as a surprise, I hired one and it landed us right at the front door! Mum was terrified, but not as terrified as she was to be with a second treat I had in store for her ... a day-trip to an exquisite hotel lodge called Wharekauhau for a posh lunch. My partner Grant and his mum Gail joined us this time, along with my sister Sue. The five of us piled into a very small helicopter to take the short ten minute flight from Wellington to Wharekauhau, which was across a mountain range. Well ... just as we were approaching the mountains the wind picked up and the little helicopter was tossing and turning, losing and gaining altitude and we were all screaming and thinking we were going to crash. It was beyond terrifying and the ordeal seemed to go on for much longer than the two minutes it actually was.

We eventually got to the hotel, landing right outside the front door – shaken and stirred – and the glass of champagne awaiting us was wildly appreciated by all. We laughed a lot about it afterwards and the meal was superb. Needless to say, we went a different way back after the lunch, along the coast, and as a treat the pilot did a sweep of the runway at Wellington airport, which was incredible.

*Dancing with the Stars* had its best season that year with over a third of the country tuning in. Its popularity had grown and grown, so it was a great shock to discover that it wasn't being recommissioned. I was sad when I found out as, apart from loving the show, it was the only time I could get together with my family and they looked forward to the yearly holidays. I think the problem was money. The show is hideously expensive to put on and there is, of course, a limited supply of celebrities. We certainly went out with a bang and on a high, and I made some really great friends at the TV station who have remained friends to this day. But like all good things, they must come to an end. I've got to thank *Strictly* for some of the most amazing experiences I've had in my life.

With my dear mum on a helicopter trip in New Zealand.

I *told* you it was a good lunch!

September inevitably saw me back in the *Strictly* fold, with a great bunch of contestants. We had the usual smattering of soap stars, some great sports stars and a couple of *Footballers' Wives* – the screen variety rather than the real thing – in Zöe Lucker and Laila Rouass.

As usual, the series wasn't without its drama – both on and off screen. There were two blossoming romances … a controversial race row … and a celebrity arrest.

In October, the press went crazy when it was alleged that Anton Du Beke had used the word 'Paki' when swapping banter with dance partner Laila – who is of Indian and Moroccan descent. It was a huge blow to the show, and the papers were full of people calling for him to be sacked. But Anton is absolutely not a racist as far as I'm concerned and he had a Japanese girlfriend at the time. Obviously, something was said, because Anton immediately apologized, but he would never have meant to say it in an offensive way. It was one of those things where she might have called herself various names, like I might call myself a 'big old poof' or 'rancid queen' – or rap stars and singers like Rihanna use the 'n' word – but if someone else says it then it's not acceptable. It was an off-the-cuff remark backstage, allegedly, so I thought he might have needed to apologize to Laila, but not to the world.

Whatever was actually said, the ensuing storm affected them both, and, in truth, there was a lot of tension between them, even though they were putting on a brave face in public.

The whole thing just highlighted how careful you have to be in public, even when you feel you are among a tightknit bunch of friends. The remark was, apparently, made in the Star Bar, the backstage area where the couples relax when they're not on set. Someone leaked it from there. There are so many people milling around and, sadly, you can't trust anyone. Look what happened to Carol Thatcher, who was pilloried in the press when she said the word 'golliwog' in the green room. It was wrong, undoubtedly, but we only know about it because someone told the press. You have to be very, very aware of what comes out of your mouth at any given point because you are surrounded by people in the media, and by people who might want to cut you down and put you in a bad light.

On a happier note, we had two passionate love affairs. Boxer Joe Calzaghe proved rather better at romancing than dancing, and swept the lovely Kristina Rihanoff off her feet – albeit not in the way the judges would have liked. And we had former *Hollyoaks* star Ali Bastion, who fell for our American boy, Brian Fortuna. It's amazing how many couples have met on the show, including Flavia Cacace and Jimi Mistri and Kara Tointon and Artem Chigvintsev, who are still together.

Being up-close-and-personal, all day every day, and working on some really sexy moves together, it's almost inevitable. A lot of ballroom and Latin dancers are husband and wife teams, because they train so often, and it's very close, it's very physical work, and you have to get quite intimate, so these things do happen. And if you're both single, then why not? Plus, it does it help in the dance department. That connection is never a bad thing during the routines.

Having said that, there wasn't much hope for Joe on the floor, but I didn't relish telling him so. I was a nervous wreck because I told him the absolute truth: he was a complete nightmare on the dance floor. No doubt at all that he put a lot of effort in, but it didn't seem like he was reaping any of the benefits. However, he did take negative comments to heart. I'm not going to lie to him and say 'fab-u-lous' when it's not, just because he's a boxer, so I just avoided him backstage! The area behind the studio is circular, so if I saw Joe coming down one corridor. I'd go the opposite way round.

There are always celebrities who take these things badly. I wish it wouldn't go further, and spill over backstage, but it does tend to because they take it personally. It's only a television show and I'm only doing a job when I'm out there. When I'm backstage I'm completely different, and that's to be expected.

Joe and Kristina's did turn into a really loving relationship but, sadly, Ali and Brian didn't last so long. They went on to star in *Burn the Floor* together, because she was a really good dancer by the end of the run. But their romance broke down in the end because, as she told me later, it always felt like a teacher–pupil relationship.

*Hollyoaks* star Ricky Whittle, with whom my mother and half the nation fell in love, had producers on the edge of their seats when he managed to get himself arrested – then spent ten hours in custody on a Friday, when the couples have their final rehearsals and get to use the studio for the first time.

Ricky Whittle charmed my mum – not that she needed much charming, she was already in love!

He had taken a night off to go back to Liverpool and attend a leaving do for one of the *Hollyoaks* cast. As he drove away, it was alleged that he swerved his car and deliberately hit a photographer. He was cleared of all charges nine months later, but the incident clouded his brilliant run on *Strictly*. He was going through all of that drama and then suddenly it wasn't about his dancing any more.

He and dance partner Natalie Lowe were a really good combination because she's such a good choreographer and willing and incredibly able. They looked absolutely delicious together and I would have put him down to win, absolutely. But Chris Hollins went on to win it, and I have no idea if Ricky's arrest had any influence on that.

In fairness, it looked like it was going Ricky's way right up to the final dances, then Chris performed such a great Charleston that he stole it. The final is all about the public vote and Chris was the underdog, which tends to endear one to the British public. Plus, as a sports presenter, he approached the training like a sportsman and worked hard, but with loads personality and cheerfulness. He was an odd one to win because you wouldn't think that the audience would vote for him, but in the end the audience are great because they end up voting for the person that dances best in the final.

Chris wasn't a crossover or a 'ten dancer', meaning someone who can dance all five ballroom and all five Latin perfectly well, whereas Ricky was brilliant at both. But sometimes the runners-up do very, very well for themselves and Ricky now lives in Hollywood and has got a good career going.

*Coronation Street* actor Craig Kelly danced with Flavia Cacace that year and he really thought he was better than he was. He got one of the best dancers in the world – the queen of Argentine tango herself – but he's probably the celebrity who took criticism the worst, apart from Jan Ravens, whose husband nearly decked me in the bar after one show.

Craig couldn't understand why I was saying what I was saying and, if I said anything negative or untoward, he would always challenge it and be gobsmacked because he thought it was all fantastic. He had a much higher opinion of himself as a dancer than any of the judges did, most certainly.

In contrast, we had the joy of Tuffers – Phil Tufnell – who took it all on the chin. He's really amenable. He is a person that the general public can associate with and they like his attitude. He wasn't a terrible dancer and he was fun because he was able to throw himself into the deep end and swim – when a lot of people sink – but also has the ability to laugh at himself. He went wrong in the dance routines an enormous number of times, but he just laughed about it. When he got criticism from the judges, he took it in good humour. 'Yeah, yeah,' he'd say. 'I need to fix that.' Or, 'Oh, I know! I went terribly wrong there, didn't I?'

Jo Wood, who had split with Rolling Stone Ronnie after years of marriage, danced with Brendan Cole and she was a delight. I don't know whether Brendan was totally up for that partnership, but Jo certainly was, and she had a great time on the show. She's very genuine, really honest, great fun and absolutely lovely to deal with. I also really liked Zöe

Lucker, who danced with James Jordan, and I thought that was a really nice combination but they never really got out of the middle of the leader board, so they only lasted until week seven.

Natalie Cassidy was a very pleasant surprise. She was really good, and she lost a load of weight. She had made a fitness video a year or so before and had shed the pounds then, but had put it all back on again. In fact, I had bumped into her some time before she was on *Strictly* in the lift at a hotel in Bristol, and I didn't recognize her. She'd been for a jog and she was going to breakfast at the hotel. She only knew me because I was a judge on *Strictly* and I only knew her from *EastEnders*, but she was so thin I didn't recognize her, and it was only when she opened her mouth to speak in the lift that I went, 'Oh my God, it's Natalie Cassidy!' She was stick thin and wearing a tiny little tank top, midriff showing, and tight little pink shorts. I couldn't believe it. She was obviously in training for that DVD at the time. But I often wonder about these DVDs, because before you do them, you've got like a three-month period to reduce weight and look fit and hot and amazing and then tell the world, 'Look what happened to me!' But it's maintaining that fitness that's the hardest thing. The pressure is immense and she told me that she wished she'd never done it.

It was an unrealistic goal, for her, as a person. Everyone

has a personal goal regarding weight and where that should be, but if you go under weight and it's unrealistic to maintain, then it's not right.

You have to devote your life to physical exercise in order to do one of those videos, and it was probably the wrong decision for her, but you sometimes think 'This will motivate me, I'll do it and then I'll keep the weight off.' But that's not the case, because you only have to stop doing it for a few days – as any ballerina will tell you – and you start to feel heavy, frumpish, clumpy and you feel like you don't have any energy.

As a sportsman, or dancer, you're essentially a racehorse, so you need constant training. We've seen how footballers – like Gazza, for example – get fat when they stop playing, because when you stop doing what you've been doing and keep eating the same you're just going to end up big. As a dancer who has struggled with weight issues all my life, I am well aware of that. But to lose weight and keep it off you need a realistic goal. *Strictly* helped her strip the weight again but, of course, when you stop dancing eight hours every day, you're going to slip back into old habits.

But Natalie was a lovely girl. Bubbly, bright and totally down to earth.

We were thrilled that year to have the beautiful long-jumper Jade Johnson, who was shaping up to be an impressive dancer. But there was more drama when she had to withdraw due to a nasty knee injury, leaving the lovely Ian Waite hanging. With the 2012 Olympics on the horizon, Jade didn't want to risk making it worse.

Professional athletes have the obvious advantage of being fit and used to training but *Strictly* is a lot harder than they might think. It can and does cause injury, and it can be dangerous. If you are still competing, it can ruin your entire professional career, so injuries have to be nursed and looked after. You wouldn't put a rugby player or football player into a game when they are badly injured, in case you damaged the ligament even more. Jade had to think about her future and I think she made the right decision to withdraw from the show but it was such a shame because she was wonderful and I thought their partnership was just really flying by week eight, which was the last dance they did. It was a long way to go to then have to leave due to injury, but it was totally unavoidable.

During the 2009 series, I got a call from QDOS Entertainment, the pantomime production people, and they said, 'We'd love you to direct one of our pantos.'

'This isn't really my genre,' I thought. 'But I suppose I could give it a go, if I had time ... Maybe.' I told them I would think about it, but being busy with *Strictly* at the same time, I left it for about a month or so. Then I got a call from Jonathan Kiley, the executive producer of QDOS, who put a rather different proposal to me. He suggested that I should be *in* the panto – as a woman!

'Oh!' I said. 'That's interesting.'

I had hung up my dancing shoes eighteen years ago and decided to just go into direction and choreography, and I never thought that I would tread the boards again. At the time, I was also overweight and the last time I had been in drag, when I performed as a divine creature called Lavish, I had a thirty-one-inch waist and I was in my twenties. The thought of digging out my high heels was exciting, but, at the same time I was thinking, 'Am I going to panic? Am I going to be able to do it?' I hadn't performed for so long, I honestly didn't know whether I'd be capable.

After mulling it over, I signed up to play the Wicked Queen in *Snow White and the Seven Dwarves* – a middle-aged woman desperate for a young man, which wouldn't be too far from the truth, I suppose!

Having accepted, I was pretty excited and felt totally up for it. But when it came to all the fittings and preparation, I went into a total spin and panicked. The frocks worried me because of my weight, and when I went for my first fitting, I just felt hideous. I had to take all my clothes off and put on a G-string, a pair of tights and a corset and I was just thinking, 'Oh my God, this is horrible. I'm mortified!'

I began to wonder if I had made the right decision and I thought, 'I'm really not fit enough to do this.'

To try to rectify the problem, I went back into training, but I wasn't losing weight quickly enough and I'd left it a bit too late. Anyway, they'd already made the frocks around me, so I was destined to be a buxom wench. In those fabulous dresses, I was like a really fat, tall Alexis Carrington Colby.

On top of the weight issues, because there was so much dialogue it took me a month to learn the lines. When I first got the script I was terrified because I had no idea how I would learn it all. My time was limited so I really had to take a month off from everything except *Strictly* just to get the lines off pat. If you're doing it all the time it's really easy, but if you're not, and you haven't had to learn lines for eighteen years, it's really quite daunting. I had imagined I would be just waltzing on, darling, in some glamorous – albeit fat – outfit, and spouting, 'Mirror, mirror on the wall, who's the fairest of them all?' But it was much, much more than that.

My wonderful PA, Clare, was a great help and would frequently say, 'Let's do your lines.' Every moment of the day I'd be studying and studying, so I could get the words imprinted on my brain and didn't have to panic about that when I went into rehearsals.

There were only ten days to rehearse – which is a really quick turnaround – and I was terribly nervous, because I didn't know whether I could do it. Everyone believed in me, but you have to believe in yourself, that's the most important thing. On the first day of rehearsal, I was so jittery about meeting everyone that all the lines went completely out of my head and I just kept saying, 'I knew this at home, I knew this at home.' It's a confidence issue and I'm extremely confident when I'm judging but when it comes to playing a role it's very different. I was also thinking, 'They'll be out to get me, because I'm putting myself in the firing line and offering myself up to critics', so that added to the nerves. There was a lot riding on it, that first year.

The show was in Llandudno in Wales and I still felt huge, despite my training regime, so the first week I was a nervous wreck. The weight fell off me throughout the run, because doing two shows a day means you burn a lot of energy.

That initial run was three weeks, because that fitted in with the *Strictly Come Dancing* schedule, and it was tiring because there was a lot of travelling. I was in London on Saturday night with *Strictly* and then I had to travel overnight to Llandudno for a performance at ten o'clock the following morning.

It's not all black-tie dinners and showbiz pizzazz, you know – a girl has to get ready!

Towards the end, I had pulled a ligament in my shoulder that was caused through repetitive strain injury and the balls of my feet were killing me, because I hadn't been in heels for years, and you forget that dancing in heels at 107 kilos – nearly seventeen stone – which I was at the time, is quite hard. Plus, I was using the wrong eyelash glue, so my eyes were swelling up and then I lost all my real eyelashes when I pulled the false ones off.

On one occasion, it was snowing and it took six hours to get up to Llandudno. I tried to sleep but it's impossible in the car, when you're ducking and diving and then going through snow, so it was really tortuous. By the time I got there it was six o'clock in the morning and I had to be in drag at eight, so I had two hours sleep and then got ready for the ten o'clock show. Unfortunately, the timings of the shows were odd because there was an evening show at seven, which meant there was a huge break in between, so I had to take my make-up off, go to the hotel, then put it all back on again and warm up, which was a nightmare.

Of course, I was right when I thought that there would be certain critics out to get me. The press – or perhaps more predictably the *Daily Mail* – were vile to me. Their review said, 'His hoofing, in one brief costume that revealed more than it was wise to show, looked as laboured as a sixty-year-old woman with varicose veins.' And they added, 'Now removed from the cover of his Saturday-night *Strictly Come Dancing* desk, Horwood is revealed to have a paunch and excess weight on his rear, a fact that not even his lavish costumes can entirely conceal.'

That wasn't thrilling me in the slightest as it was in a double-page spread, but like all these things you've got to sit back and laugh. I got some good reviews but it was clear some people were just getting me back for being Mr Nasty on TV. It was an opportunity for them to see me sing and dance and they were using that as an excuse to lash out. Maybe I *was* fat and horrible with varicose veins, but most of the audiences loved it and it sold out every night, so QDOS Entertainment invited me back to do it again the following year. And spending most of my waking hours in drag made for a very interesting Christmas.

# CHAPTER 2

# HIGHS AND LOWS

For the *Strictly Come Dancing Live* tour, the following January, the production company, Phil McIntyre Entertainment, brought Arlene back into the fold, as the director. She had successfully forged the first show the year before and, despite being axed from the main series, had agreed to return for a final hurrah.

'You can take the girl out of *Strictly*, but you can't take *Strictly* out of the girl,' she said.

This year, Len couldn't do every show, so Arlene stood in as honorary head judge and, of course, it was lovely to have her back, but Bruno and I did a lot of whingeing because our scripts had to keep changing all the time. It was slightly weird having Arlene on the panel, as if we hadn't done the entire TV series without her, but the audience absolutely loved it. The round of applause she got coming down the stairs was deafening and she got to hand out the glitterball trophy at the end.

On this tour, Kelly Brook, who had been a wonderful dancer but had left series five when her father sadly passed away, returned to dance with Matt Cutler, and series six contestant Austin Healey paired up with Lilia Kopylova, and the series four champ Mark Ramprakash was with Kristina Rihanoff.

The rest were from the last series, so we had Ali Bastion and Brian Fortuna, Chris Hollins and Ola Jordan, Zöe Lucker and James Jordan, Ricky Groves and Aliona Vilani, and Natalie Cassidy with Darren Bennett.

It was really wonderful to have Kelly back and watch her recreate her dance numbers in full, because she was absolutely fantastic, and she's gorgeous, plus she's a genuinely nice girl. Ali and Brian were going strong at that point in their relationship, so that added some fire to the dance floor. Chris was a laugh, and hugely popular, and Mark Ramprakash was a massive hit with the ladies.

Joe Calzaghe, who wasn't in the show, came along to be with Kristina but he was a bit jealous of Mark, who was her dance partner. They did his trademark salsa, which was quite sexy, but Kristina was always a bit wary of getting too close, in case Joe got jealous – and Mark was a bit nervous too. They had to make sure they danced as far apart as possible.

Natalie Cassidy was a sweetheart, as always, and the audience liked her. But we had no inkling that, throughout the tour, she was pregnant. We toured through January and February and, in March, she announced she was twelve weeks pregnant. It must have been tough for her because you need a lot of energy for those shows, but she never let on at all.

Zöe Lucker was just great to work with, really professional, totally down to earth. She had a bit of hang up because she never thought she was good enough. Actually, she was really, really good, but she didn't believe in herself as much as I thought she could.

The comic turn of the show was Ricky Groves. He was always up for a laugh and he was always game to answer back, which I like, but he also wanted to use the tour to learn to dance better. He came on in leaps and bounds but, because everyone else did, too, he remained at the bottom of the leader board. At times, he was upset by our comments. After one show, he said, 'Oh, I see, is this the way it's going?'

'Well no, it depends how you dance,' I said. 'If you dance brilliantly then we'll be kind, but if there's anything wrong, we're going to point it out.' But he could take the mickey out of himself at the expense of good dancing and it was brilliant that he was able to turn the whole routine into a comedy one and have the audience in fits.

Even though the couples are doing the same dances, the standard can differ night to night. We have big parties on tour and they say, 'What goes on tour stays on tour,' but I can tell you we party a *lot* and then the couples have to come in and dance the next day. It's all right for me. I'm just sitting at the desk slagging people off: or 'offering honest advice', as I prefer to call it – but the celebs have to do something physical. Believe me, nursing a hangover while trying to do those dance routines on a matinée day is not a good look!

Austin Healey and James Jordan were unbelievably naughty together on that tour. They are both jokers, always punching each other, wrestling in the dressing room, and generally getting into trouble. There was always something going on, and James was goading Austin the whole time. It always ended in something stupid happening – in a light-hearted way. They were terrible practical jokers. They kept tying everyone's shoelaces together and swapping the costumes around in the quick change areas, which is a pain because people have literally minutes to whip on a new outfit backstage and any delay can cause a panic. The male judges shared a big dressing room and on one occasion we came back in to the green room after a show to find all the furniture – sofa and all – had disappeared from the room. They had put them all down in the boys' dressing room. Daft stunts like that were occurring every day. There are always one or two jokers in the pack.

At the end of my last book, *All Balls and Glitter*, I was head over heels in love with my then partner Grant and wondering if I had finally found my soulmate. It was early days and we wanted to see where it took us ... and we had four years together, the first two of which were fantastic.

Grant and I met online and had a few dates before I was due to go to New Zealand for two months, to film *Dancing with the Stars*. I was crazy about him so, when the lease on his flat was coming to an end, I told him it would be daft to go house-hunting.

'Come to New Zealand,' I said. 'We can spend two months together there and, if that all goes well, you can stay at mine when we get back.' So that's what happened and, after a brilliant eight weeks, he moved in to my little palace. On reflection, it was probably too quick. We had only known each other three months by then and, although it was pretty intense, we should maybe have put the brakes on. For that, I blame myself.

It had been two years since my split with Lloyd, my long-term boyfriend, and I had been so used to living with him and having someone around all the time, for all those years, I must have wanted to fill that void. That is probably why I jumped in with both feet when I met Grant. We got on very, very well – like a house on fire – and he was a lot quieter than me so that calmed me down and settled me a bit.

For the first two years we had a ball. Then things began to go downhill a bit and it all came to a head when we went on holiday with my sister, Susan, and her husband, David, in the summer of 2010. We flew out to the beautiful island of Santorini, in Greece, and the surroundings couldn't have been more romantic and picturesque, but something just wasn't right. It seemed like Grant and I were on different holidays, and wanted different things from the experience.

My life is quite busy and stressful and the only way I can get away from work, emails and phone calls is to go away, so when I take a break, I just like to relax in the sunshine. I like to have a nice glass of Sauvignon Blanc with my lunch, I like to swim and sunbathe and sometimes have a little wander somewhere in the afternoon and then go out for a leisurely dinner. That's how I unwind.

Grant really wasn't into the long, boozy lunches and wanted a more active time, which is fair enough. But he'd have a sparkling mineral water and then going off exploring by himself, while I stayed by the pool, so I knew it wasn't going particularly well.

As a special treat, I hired a yacht one day and I thought he'd enjoy that. But he didn't like the idea of a day's sailing and, although he agreed to come, he was in the cabin most of the time. 'Come up the front and enjoy the spray,' I said, but he just wasn't budging.

That would all have been fine but he started voicing concerns about me to my sister, and telling her a lot of personal stuff that he had never talked to me about. It soon became clear that the communication in the relationship was breaking down, that we weren't actually talking to one another enough about our feelings. Instead of causing friction, we had been leaving things to lie dormant, sweeping all the little niggles that are inevitable in a relationship under the carpet so as to avoid confrontation. So he was pouring it all out to Sue, and she was coming back to me and telling me what he'd said and I was pretty hurt by some of the comments.

In one comment, it was suggested that I was full of myself! As anyone else who knows me would tell you, this is not true of me at all. I'm very grounded, I'm very down to earth and I hope I'm a very generous person. I've been working in this business for so long now and, by necessity, you become hardened to all the showbiz pizzazz. After ten years on TV, you don't go out to celebrity functions 'full of yourself' and I'm very careful to live a normal life away from the screen. Some people enjoy the whole thing about being a celebrity – the opening night parties and the premières – but I tend to shy away from most of those events.

When I do walk down the red carpet, I'm aware that I have to be quite vibrant and answer a lot of questions, and there are always a million interviews and a lot of flash photography but Grant seemed to enjoy that side of it. He was very nervous the first time he was by my side at one of these events, and kept asking, 'What do I do? What do I do?'

'Just stay next to me,' I said. 'You'll be fine.' People are a bit overwhelmed when they're in that situation for the first time, and so his first red carpet was probably a nightmare for him, but he soon started to get used to it and was becoming good at handling that side of our lives. Actually, I thought the relationship was going well. He had been really great at dealing with both the celebrity nature of the relationship – which is difficult enough – but also my personal side, which is totally different.

Don't get me wrong, I do like to party, but I still like to have a bit of quiet time as well. Unfortunately, Grant's quiet time was a bit *too* quiet for me. He would often be in bed by 9.30. He may have been younger than me but, as he said himself, he was more like the grandfather in the relationship, with the slippers and the dressing gown and saying, 'Come up to bed' at nine o'clock.

'No thanks,' I'd say. 'I'm wide awake.' My curfew is more like midnight, and that's when I start considering bed. I only sleep for about six hours a night, and if I went to bed at nine o'clock I'd be up at some ungodly hour in the morning not knowing what to do with myself. I get a lot more achieved in my life if I stay up late, answering emails and working on shows. And if you're dealing with America, which I frequently am, it makes more sense to work later because the time difference means that calls start coming in at seven o'clock in the evening. My working day is definitely not nine-to-five, and Grant wasn't used to that.

Anyway, all these little things began to add up and, during the Santorini holiday, after my sister had heard his gripes, she asked: 'Are you telling me all this stuff about Craig because you want me to go back and tell him?'

'No, no, don't do that,' he protested. But I suspect that's what he wanted. In the end, he did tell me himself, after Sue and David left to go home. We had one extra night on the island by ourselves and I decided to take the bull by the horns.

'Listen, Grant, I'm not sure we are completely compatible together,' I said, as we sat over dinner. 'When I'm on holiday

I like to relax and enjoy my time off, but we never want to do the same things.' Of course, that was a tiny part of the issue but holidays do tend to bring problems into sharp focus.

As soon as I'd said my piece, Grant started crying – and that started me off. We were in the most romantic setting, and there we were, crying over our dinner the whole time! We really didn't know what to do. We could talk and talk and talk about it, but he's the type of person who doesn't give a lot away, and is not very comfortable with communicating his feelings and emotions. Dealing as I do with actors and dancers, I'm used to people expressing their emotions on a daily basis and I tend to be forward at saying how I feel but I hadn't been laying my cards on the table either.

So we spent the evening talking about us and I told him, 'When we get back home, we need to take a good look at the relationship and see where we go from here.'

Inevitably, though, we slipped straight back into our joint lives and it was another six months before the cracks started to show again. Then I started to think that we really needed to find a solution if this was going to work. I felt there was an imbalance in our relationship but it took me a while to put my finger on it. Then it struck me that I instigated just about everything we did. That may seem controlling, but it wasn't that way at all. It was just that so much of my life is pre-arranged and pre-organized – with meetings, opening nights, interviews, TV recordings etc. – and the rare nights that I have free I then tend to mix with my friends, because otherwise I would never see them. I suppose it was sometimes difficult slotting time with Grant into all of that, but when we were together, I realized, it was always me who suggested what we should do.

For example, on a free Saturday or Sunday, I would say, 'Let's go on a bike ride up to Hampstead Heath and have a picnic,' so we would do just that, and have a lovely day. But Grant never came up with a suggestion like that for me and for three years I hardly noticed how much I was organizing in the relationship. Even sex was always instigated by me and by the time I had worked all this out, there were a lot of underlying issues accumulating that we never spoke about.

He was desperately unhappy at work, and we spoke about that, but he never said, 'I'm unhappy in the relationship because of this or because of that.' We let it go on for so long that there was no way back. I knew that, but he had to discover that by himself, so for the last six months we were together, I took the conscious decision to organize nothing. I didn't arrange dinners, I didn't arrange days out, holidays or anything. I just stopped taking the lead, just to see what would happen – and nothing did.

Through those six months, we grew further and further

apart. We never spoke about it and I found it really difficult to bring it up because we were so settled together in the house. Grant was a great home-maker, he was fantastic, and he got into cooking, which was wonderful. His favourite thing to do was to make millions of cupcakes, and that gave him a hobby and kept him occupied if I had to go away or was working a lot. He became the home bake queen but meanwhile our relationship went distinctly off the boil. We ended up in a platonic relationship, living side by side.

Grant suffers from depression and I have to admit I don't deal with that very well. On one occasion, I came into the house and he was just sitting in the base of the shower in the dark, with the water running over his head. I'd come home and find him in these very dark despairing moments and I just couldn't communicate with him.

I've never been with anyone who's had depression and it's a difficult thing for me to understand because, despite my *Strictly* persona, I'm a very upbeat person. I know a lot of people suffer from depression and I knew I had to be very careful with how I handled it, so I didn't want to bring any problems to the table at a time when he was really suffering. It wasn't always easy to tell when that was because, as he told me himself, he would often pretend to be happy by trying to mask the depression. He told me he had been doing that for years, and I didn't even pick up on it. I thought that he was happy, but deep down inside he was suffering in silence and alone and, of course, that's awful.

Because I had no experience of depression, it was quite an eye-opener, so I decided in the last six months just to sort of go easy and let *him* make up his own mind, let him see what the relationship was and what it wasn't.

In March 2010, we went on holiday to the Maldives, which was absolutely gorgeous and idyllic. On Bruno Tonioli's recommendation, we stayed at the Centura Grand Hotel Resort and Spa. Bruno is now officially my holiday guru, and where he hasn't been is nobody's business.

We flew business class into Male, then took a seaplane transfer to the resort. It was like being on a film set, everything was perfect white sand, blue lagoon. It was like living in a tropical fish tank – so perfect it all looked manmade, like Disneyland. The restaurants were amazing, our luxury sunset villa was to die for and we had our very own house on stilts with two balconies you could just dive right off, and into the warm tropical clear waters, and swim with the incredible array of tropical fish – it was unbelievable. The toilet had a glass floor so you see the fish below. Now I know why couples go there on their honeymoons. It's so romantic and peaceful. It isn't cheap, mind you, but worth every penny. We mainly lazed around the beaches or lay by the pool drinking cocktails most days. It's not an adventure holiday, it's very quiet and the island is small – you can walk around it in twenty minutes – ideal for Granty and me.

We were chatting to our fellow holidaymakers at the resort and Grant met a young couple who were on their honeymoon. He got on particularly well with the bride – who had been with her new husband for ten years before they wed – and he told me she was already having problems in the marriage.

'Oh, my God,' I said 'Really? They're on their honeymoon!' It sounded like a nightmare in the Maldives – the most beautiful place and expensive place in the world and the honeymoon has gone wrong. Anyway, Grant and the bride became really good friends and she became someone that he could confide in, so they met up after we got home.

One Sunday, after we got back, I woke up with a rare free day ahead of me. 'OK, so what have you got planned for me today?' I asked Grant.

'Oh, I hadn't really thought about it,' he said. 'We could go out for a pizza or go for a bike ride.' That sounded like what I would normally suggest so I waited to see if there was anything else. Then he added, 'Or I could cook a roast for lunch.'

'Yes, great idea,' I said. 'What meat shall we have?' I was determined he was making all the decisions, even the little tiny domestic decisions like that – but then you discover a lot about people in that domesticity and when the relationship has changed the little things stand out. So I felt I couldn't help him choose, because he had to see clearly for himself how often I *did* make the decisions.

'I'll go down to Sainsbury's,' he said, and off he went, leaving me looking forward to a home-cooked roast.

An hour passed, and then another, and I thought he was taking an awfully long time to come back. I texted him several times but no reply, and I thought, 'This is odd'. By three in the afternoon there was still no sign and I was waiting for lunch to arrive.

'The supermarket is five minutes away and he left four hours ago!' I thought. 'Something's up here, but I'm not going to waste my Sunday afternoon off.'

I tried to ring, but got his voicemail, so I decided to take a walk round Camden Market, which I hadn't done for years. I wandered around for a while and came back home about five o'clock in the afternoon. Still no sign of Grant.

Not long after that, he came home.

'Where have you been?' I asked. I was trying not be too demanding, but I was upset, because I didn't know what was going on. He was really quiet and went into the bedroom and I looked in and said, 'What's wrong? What's happening?'

He told me that he'd been out for lunch with his friend,

the bride from the Maldives holiday, and I said, 'Oh, I see. I thought we were having lunch together?'

'Oh, no,' he said. 'Didn't you get my text message?'

'No,' I said. 'I didn't. But I thought we were having lunch together,'

'Well, the bride called and we went out for lunch,' he said. 'We had a lot of talking to do.'

It would normally be about her relationship, but this time it seemed he was talking to her about *his* relationship and problems we had, instead of talking to me.

'I've been speaking to her about relationship stuff,' he added.

'What relationship?' I asked, knowing full well.

'Well, ours,' he answered, a little sheepishly.

'OK,' I said. 'Why don't you speak to *me* about our relationship rather than telling her because that's the only way to solve it.'

Grant was getting more and more upset and then he said the one thing he had been gearing up for all afternoon.

'I really – I think I just need – my own space at the moment.'

'OK. What does that mean?' I asked.

'Well, I just – you know, I just – I need to have my own space.'

'Oh, right, we're splitting up, are we? Is that the thing?'

'Well I'm ...' Grant trailed off. He doesn't like anything confrontational and it was a big decision that he had made, but I felt the weight fall from my shoulders.

It was a huge relief that he had made the decision and that I was happy with that decision, because I'd always felt he needed to find himself and grow as a person.

Looking back, he was probably just a bit young, although he was twenty-nine when I met him, and he wasn't really ready for this particular relationship.

So that was it. Grant had made a positive decision, and I could only see positivity coming from it, rather than heartache. Those first two years I had been really happy, starting anew and getting Lloyd completely out of my system. It was a loving relationship and to this day we still love each other very much, but we really should not be together, and we established that, without doubt, in those last six months.

We have spoken about it since, and he agreed that he was very unhappy in his job, he didn't know where he was in life, he wasn't completely happy living in my shadow and wanted to be more of himself. The only way he was going to discover that was by moving out and living a life without me.

Initially, to save too much turmoil from having to move out immediately, I suggested he could stay with me for a while, but using the spare room. I'm out a lot and he could have his own space, his own wardrobes and so on, so we agreed on that. But for two weeks he locked himself away in that bedroom, and it was really difficult to communicate. It was difficult for both of us because we were so used to sleeping in the same bed, sharing the same room and cooking dinner together. I've never lived with someone I've split up with and it was a bit awkward. But it was a learning curve. I was just trying to make his transition easier for him.

After an extensive search – because he likes his luxury and home comforts – Grant found a place that he was very excited about and moved out. When he left my overwhelming feeling was relief, again, but only for Grant, because I wanted him to be happy. I wanted him to be well and enjoy his life and I didn't want to hamper that in any way through selfish concerns. In the end it was right that we had to let each other go.

Initially, Grant found the transition quite difficult because I'd always been there for him, I was his support, I was the daddy in the relationship, because he was fifteen years younger than me. I suppose that taught me a bit of a lesson as well, because you do often think, 'Should I be with someone who is that much younger?' Age gaps don't always matters. It depends on the people involved. But he needed to learn a lot more and become his own man.

When he first moved out he got a flatmate, which was good for him, because he was used to having someone to come home to. A year later, he has his own place, and is completely independent again. I think that's very important before you're with anybody else – you have to love yourself first before you give your entire heart and soul away to someone else again.

Despite the split, Grant and I remained close. We had turned into mates in the last six months of the relationship, so it wasn't as if anything had changed except we weren't living together. The thing that we both missed more than anything was the cuddles – that reassuring hug when you're worried or need a bit of reassurance. That's the worst thing to lose.

Grant and I were in love at the start, but it ended up being a platonic relationship that was completely devoid of any sex. Now we can laugh about that, because we've had a year and a half away from one another, and enough time to heal, so we can come back together and look at the lovely times we had. I made him photo books of our relationship – not to bind it and then throw it away, but just to remember the fun times that we had and to look back on it and say, 'That was great while it lasted.' It was a good learning curve, it helped us both grow and we needed one another at the time. I think people often come together at the time that they need each other and then when that runs out, it runs out. I don't know if I'll ever find anyone who is going to be there for ever but I no longer expect that.

In the summer of 2010, I was at the Watermill Theatre, directing *Copacabana*, when I began working secretly with Andrew Lloyd Webber on a plan to fix his ailing musical, *Love Never Dies*. The Watermill is very close to Sydmonton, his beautiful estate, and the year before Andrew had come to see my production of *Sunset Boulevard*, as did the show's lyricist Don Black. To my relief, both had loved it.

That show was a critical success and transferred to the West End, to rave reviews.

The show consisted of twelve actor/singers who were also the musicians – we call them actor/musos in the industry. I have always considered *Sunset Boulevard* to be a chamber piece that would lend itself to that kind of treatment. It was originally directed by me at the Watermill Theatre in Newbury, which is an extremely intimate space with an audience capacity of two hundred, so a West End transfer of the show needed to take that into consideration. It transferred to the Comedy Theatre (now renamed The Harold Pinter Theatre), which has a really intimate stage, making it perfect environment for *Sunset*. Despite many glowing reviews, the show sadly didn't get enough bums on seats and closed earlier than expected, which was a terrible shame, as I would've liked more people to see the incredible cast we had and for potential audiences to know it was a very different version from the big bravado original.

I have worked with Andrew on many a project and I really love and admire him. He's a genius. He's also a very sweet guy and we get on like a house on fire.

In 2010, he wanted me to take over and redirect *Love Never Dies*, which already had a scarred and tawdry past, and was completely limping in the West End. I was meant to come in as a 'theatre doctor' and fix it up a little bit and then take it to Toronto and Australia. We worked on it over a six-month period at Sydmonton, trying to solve all the problems. They'd had a team from America to do it originally, but they just wanted to help it evolve, and re-create it while it was still on, while the set was still there, while the people were still there and while the theatre was still available. I agreed to it, because I thought, 'I do have an opinion on it and I really can change it'. Then I spoke to Andrew about it at length and discussed how we could improve it, how we could re-think it and how it could be re-staged.

I was to have a two-week rehearsal period where I would implement my changes, which would then go into the

London production, and then, out of that would come a production in Toronto and then a production in Australia. However, after working on it for a while, Andrew said he wanted me to co-direct the Melbourne production with the Australian director, Simon Phillips.

'I really don't think that would work,' I told him. 'I'm very heavily set on my version of it and I don't know that I can share that out.' Sadly, it then transpired the producers couldn't get the funding in Toronto so I said I wasn't interested in doing the changes in the West End.

Toronto was to have been my reward for the London revamp, the place where I could put my own version on from day one. I wasn't keen to do only the West End changes, because I was doctoring something that had already been doctored umpteen times by so many directors and choreographers, by friends of mine. I just thought it was bad form. So we pulled the plug two weeks before I was meant to start rehearsals. In the end, Bill Kenwright took over in the West End and Simon did a fantastic job in Melbourne.

The whole episode was disappointing because I'd been working on it for six months, and I loved the music and was excited about the project. It's not easy to work out what's fair in love and war when you don't actually see the project through, and that was largely due to the fact that contracts and various other elements weren't in place at the right time for us to go forward with it.

I loved the show and I just wanted to be able to make it better, and I'd worked hard with Andrew to try and recreate it, but I think it's better that it went to someone completely different and someone Australian to try it out somewhere else.

I have great respect for Andrew, because he's a fantastic talent and, as I say, I love him as a person as well. We get very excitable together and spark off one another, and I thought it a great shame not to fulfil our dream for the show. But you can't get your heart set on something and then be disappointed if it doesn't work out, not in this industry. You've got to have the skin of a rhinoceros and take it as it comes, because not everything works out.

Now I'm a producer myself, I understand what it's like to put money in and then to have it fail – and you don't want that. You're always hoping that that money will lead to a success or lead to more employment in the theatre and keep theatre alive, but sometimes it's just not to be.

# CHAPTER 3

# BANGERS AND CLASH

The next series of *Strictly* brought us the usual thrills and spills – and an odd exchange between myself and Paul Daniels which resulted in 'Sausage-gate'.

The musically challenged magician had conjured Ola Jordan from a magic box on stage before delivering a dreadful cha-cha-cha, so I said, 'The best thing about that dance was the empty box'.

Paul answered back with, 'Don't give up your day job tasting sausages!' And all hell broke loose. Everyone watching assumed he was being homophobic. In fact, as I pointed out on Twitter, Paul had been referring to my being crowned King of the Sizzle for British Sausage Week, a few days before. And because I took the crown from him, as he'd been the previous year's official sausage taster, he was making a little jibe about it.

In the aftermath of the comment, though, Paul kept digging himself into a hole as he tried to defend himself with that favourite old line, 'I've got a lot of gay friends'. But that put him in even worse stead. He was voted out of the show two weeks later, in week three.

Sausage Week itself, in November, was hilarious. As Sizzle King, my task was to travel around the country in a sausage van, handing out awards for the best sausages. There was a winner for each region, but one overall winner and that was the London-based one.

I thought the van was going to have a huge sausage on the top of it, but when I turned up for tasting duty on the first day, I was delighted to see it was a normal white van that we sat in the back of as we travelled to various tastings. We started at eight o'clock in the morning, munching our way through a whole variety of different bangers and ticking off whether they were firm, whether they cut nicely, whether they split, fat to meat content etc. I must have eaten two hundred sausages that week – as well as dancing with a great big banger at a shopping centre. I literally had to waltz with a sausage!

To the victor, the spoils! A round of applause for your Sizzle King.

Series nine of *Strictly* also saw the unforgettable arrival of Ann Widdecombe, our very first politician. And, boy, did she make an impact! Her dancing with Anton Du Beke had the world in stitches and she went from Tory battle-axe to comedy queen with their hilarious routines.

There was a bit of a scandal in the papers when Jimi Mistry and dance partner Flavia Cacace became an item, because no one was really sure if she'd split from Matt Di Angelo, whom she had also met on the show. But Jimi and Flavia are very much in love and about to get married, so good luck to them. Jimi is a lovely guy and we became great friends. I really respect him and he's a person I can go out and have a beer with and we always have a good time.

When I heard Michelle Williams was going to be on the show, I thought she was going to be fantastic. Coming from Destiny's Child, dancing with Beyoncé and all that, you would think she would be incredible … but she was quite dreadful. As sweet as she is, her lack of dancing ability was a bit shocking.

Goldie was with Kristina Rihanoff and he was also a shock. He being a DJ and musician, we expected great things, but it was really odd because he could obviously hear the rhythm but it didn't translate to the feet. So he was first to go.

Felicity Kendall was a delight to have on the show and we were very lucky to have someone of that stature and glamour, and someone the nation loves so much. A true lady.

I got on well with Patsy Kensit but, as was reported and known at the time, she was very emotionally fragile. She took criticism to heart, because she was suffering a confidence crisis in her personal life, after splitting up with her husband. She was a bit paranoid about the dancing and she wasn't completely free with it. Although she wanted to do a good job, she was always judging herself. While that's no bad thing, you have to be fair on yourself as well.

On one occasion, she got very excited because I liked one of her dance routines. In the bar afterwards, she was beside herself and kept saying, 'Oh, thank you, thank you.'

'Don't thank me,' I said. 'Thank yourself, darling. You're the one who actually achieved it and you're the one who came through from the dance gutter up to the pavement and on to the upper echelons.'

Sometimes you have a good day, sometimes you have a bad day, but she obviously had a good day that day.

Patsy was dancing with Robin Windsor, and he dealt with her brilliantly. Sometimes celebs who are anxious about performing can become so panicky that it's really difficult to teach them, and as well as being the teacher, our professional becomes the doctor, the psychiatrist, the emotional sounding board, the nurturer, the carer, the mother, the father, the sister, the brother, the support. It can be quite draining for them.

At one point, Robin took me aside and said, 'Go easy on Patsy.' But I had to explain to him that I've got to be honest and I've got to tell the truth. Just because someone's a little bit fragile, I can't *not* tell them what's wrong with their dancing.

This was the first year for Robin and Artem, and my good friends Ian Waite and Matt Cutler were ousted. I think the BBC was after some hot, young beefcake, and those two certainly had the muscle. Ian stayed within the *Strictly* fold, as a lot of them have. Matt, I imagine, didn't want to. I haven't really spoken to him about it, but I see Ian all the time in *It Takes Two* and he has choreographed the tours, so I have a closer relationship him.

Gavin Henson was very sweet. He was a very good-looking chap, and he seemed very nice, although we didn't get a lot of emotion out of him – I would like to have seen a bit more personality. I thought Scott Maslin was fabulous in the semi-finals, just brilliant. He came out and did a fantastic jive. Sadly, he never got any further but then when you look at the three finalists – Pamela Stephenson, Matt Baker and Kara Tointon – they were three fantastic dancers.

Of course, Kara's dream came true. *Strictly Come Dancing* changed her life, for ever. She's getting all the acting work that she's ever wanted, it re-kicked and re-booted her career to such an extent that people now notice her as an actress, and not just a character from *EastEnders*. She is the toast of the West End – and soon she'll be moving into movies, I'm sure. And, in Artem, she got her dream man out of it too. They're a beautiful couple and it's one of those real-life fairytales. They both found love, they found fame, they found fortune, they found it all.

After my first-ever panto run, in Llandudno, I had vowed never to drag up again, but when QDOS asked me to do it the following year, in Crawley, I thought, 'At least it's closer to home. That's much more manageable.' The Wicked Queen was set to rise again.

This time, I had more of an idea of what I was doing and I got into training a lot earlier. I went to the gym for two months before and got fit because I knew what was expected of me. Crawley was a much nicer experience because of that – apart from the fact that I lost my voice halfway through.

I picked up a bout of flu and I was literally shaking on stage. I was staying in a Holiday Inn next to the theatre and the only place I could eat was at the local Harvester, so I would have my food there and then go to bed. I confined myself to bed for a week and just got up and did the two shows every single day, but it was exhausting and my voice went. I still had to sing all the numbers so I sounded like Barry White doing *Snow White and the Seven Dwarves*.

Most of the run went smoothly except for one time, when I skipped an entire scene and I was calling for Snow White – and she was on the toilet! I was screaming, 'Snow White! Summon Snow White!' and she was upstairs, nowhere near the stage. There were loud stage whispers of 'It's the dog bit next!' coming from everyone in the wings and our starring pooch, Churchill the dog, was waiting to come on. I was thinking, 'What are they talking about? I've just introduced

Snow White.' Then it suddenly struck me that I'd left out the entire scene.

So I told the audience, 'Oh, she's obviously not coming on. But anyway, shall we speak to Churchill, my dog?' It made it look like she was the one who was at fault, when I was entirely to blame, which was naughty of me.

That year was the first year I directed the *Strictly* tour and I wanted to make it as theatrical as possible. I made the band more visible on stage and introduced the audience to the vocalists, who are incredibly talented. I also put a raised platform in the centre to highlight the dancing because, of course, it's a massive floor on which to perform and because it's so enormous, some of the dancing, particularly if there's just a couple on there, gets lost. This focussed the dancing on one space that split apart at the end, then we got the formation dancers and – to bring some seriously silly stuff into the show – Ann and I did our Charleston in the open space.

Series eight finalists Kara Tointon, Matt Baker and Pamela Stephenson all came along as did Jimi Mistry, but without his Flavia, who was off doing a show with her professional partner Vincent Simone. Series three contestant Colin Jackson came back and series seven runner-up, the extremely talented Ricky Whittle, finally got his chance to do the live show, having missed out the year before because of a big storyline in *Hollyoaks*.

There was some real talent on that tour, but Matt and Aliona Vilani lifted the trophy most nights and broke the record for tour wins, with 26 out of the 35.

At the beginning of the tour, my comedy section with Ann was a struggle because, as I mentioned, I was pretty unfit. Ann had a running gag about my weight because I was quite big, but then as the tour went on, because I was dancing every night, I lost about two stone. It got to the stage that the fat jokes weren't working any more because I was actually getting thinner and thinner. Ann even said to me, 'Every day you come in you're slimmer.' 2

'That's because I'm running around the arena to get to you,' I said. The routine may have only been two minutes but it's very high octane, and energetic and, while it didn't matter what she did, I had to dance well. I remember one of the former professional dancers, Karen Hardy, coming up to me at the end of the O2 performance, and praising me for getting up and having a go, which gave me a feeling of exhilaration. Now I know what it feels like to be a contestant, and receiving the approval they crave.

Perhaps I'll be nicer next year. Or not!

# CHAPTER 4

# A LIGHT GOES OUT

Since we met some twenty years ago, when I was still getting used to living in London, Amber has been as close as a friend could be. In the early years, we had some pretty wild times together and, when she settled down with her husband, Mark, and had children, I became godfather to her first son, Monty Revel – whose middle name was used after me. Grant is godfather to her second, Digby Rollo, and our old friend Magatha is godfather to her daughter, Beatrix Belle.

In the early summer, 2010, Amber and Mark invited Grant and me round for Sunday lunch. She was heavily pregnant with her fourth child, a girl they had already named Matilda, and after the initial pleasantries, in typically blunt style, she told us that she had cancer and only had a few months to live.

She hadn't been feeling well throughout the pregnancy,

but the pregnancy had masked all of the symptoms and she had put it down to morning sickness, wind or indigestion. When she was six months in, they discovered that she had cancer of the colon and cancer of the liver, and that it had now spread to her lung. The doctors said that she probably wouldn't reach the full term of her pregnancy. It came as a huge shock to all of us because she looked amazingly well. She was gorgeous and, we had thought, blooming in pregnancy. She looked absolutely beautiful, which made this dreadful news even harder to take in.

Amber was a wonderful friend to me for many years and I'm proud to be godfather to her son, Monty Revel.

As she was only forty-one, she thought that maybe, if she could get treatment, she would have a chance to live a bit longer, so the decision was made that she would try to prolong her life through chemotherapy and radiotherapy, but that meant terminating the pregnancy at six months. It was deeply traumatic, because she had to give birth to Matilda, and then she and Mark had to go through the naming, the funeral and cremation of their beautiful baby girl. If that wasn't difficult enough, she had two sons and a daughter, all under the age of five, who she knew she would soon be leaving behind, which broke her heart.

After Matilda's funeral, she started treatment and that gave her another three months to live on top of the three they had predicted. She was hoping that the treatment might have given her longer, because there were new cures coming along all the time. Sadly, she went through the chemo and radiotherapy but it didn't slow the cancer down enough to save her. It just gave her a little extra time so she could fix everything in life and leave it all in order.

As well as being a great mother, she was an astute businesswoman and was running a business with Mark. She was the brains, who dealt with the business side, and he did the practical stuff. And together they made a great team.

She was still positive to the end and still hopeful. She

refused to go into palliative care. She hated the idea of it because she knew that that's where they send people to die. She was still vibrant of mind, and determined to live at home as much as she could, to be with the children. She put all her effort into getting well, but unfortunately fate wasn't on her side.

Grant was working with cancer patients at University College Hospital at the time, and she found in him a great support. He had a network of people talk to, and he made sure she was getting the best care possible. He used to go round there by himself and sit with her, explaining what was going on and reassuring her, so that brought them quite close together.

The horror was that, towards the end, she just wanted to stay alive until she was forty-two, because her mother had gone exactly the same way when she was forty-one, and Amber didn't want her daughter to grow up thinking that she's going to get cancer and die at the same age. She prayed that she would break that cycle and at least get to her forty-second birthday. Tragically, she died the week before her birthday.

It was a terrible loss for everyone and what Mark was going through must have been absolutely enormous because, not only did he have to look after the business, but he had three young children and he was mourning the love of his life. It was just absolutely horrific.

Amber's birthday, 8 November, had always been a huge deal and we called it Ambi-day. As long as I'd known her, she had always had a party and would be most upset with friends if they didn't celebrate her birthday in proper style, because, she told everybody, 'You can't forget Ambi-day!' Mark thought it fitting that her funeral was on Ambi-day, so we were all given tasks to do to help him out because it was such an enormous thing to arrange. I did a board and poster for the crematorium, with a beautiful picture of her on her wedding day, and Grant made this amazing 'Amber' sign on clear Perspex, studded with Swarovski crystals, which was just beautiful.

Mark took the children to the paint store and they chose the pink paint for the coffin because her favourite colour was pink, and we said goodbye to her in a beautiful, but extremely sad, way. Mark tried to hold it together but, of course, it was impossible and he broke down during the service.

Amber and Mark had met at a gay club called the Black Cap in Camden Town. Mark had been head chef at The Engineer, where Lloyd and I both worked as waiters and, after work one night, we all went to the Black Cap and Amber came and met us. She and Mark hit it off immediately – and, in fact, they were told off for snogging and rolling about on the bar. The barman told them, 'This is a gay place, not a straight place, and could you please stop snogging!'

It felt only right that we should have her wake at the Black Cap where their love story began. Also, she loved Bunny Boys and Bunny Girls and had them at every party she ever had, so we booked out the Black Cap for that particular afternoon and we hired Bunny Boys and Bunny Girls to come and serve all the drinks and canapés. We played a selection of all the songs that Amber loved, like Barry Manilow, and we put a big poster of her on the stage, and lit it up, with Grant's crystalized sign. Everyone remembered her in a fun spirited, amazing way – and Amber would have thoroughly approved.

When it was all over, Mark had to get on with his life and deal with the kids, and I remember Amber saying, 'Please, please, whatever you do, make sure that the kids get a good education, don't forget their birthdays and make sure they're OK at Christmas.' So I try to get over as much as I can and, at Christmas, I go and see their Nativity play at school. But Mark is coping incredibly well with his life now. He had so much to deal with, with the business, the kids, finding nannies and so on but he's got on really well.

Monty's growing up to be a really intelligent and wonderful boy. Digby loves ballet and dancing, and Trixie is the spitting image of Amber. When I saw her in the Nativity play, last Christmas, I just wept. I sat there just crying my eyes out, but it's just wonderful that she's got that legacy, that she does have a family.

Another constant reminder of Amber is my car – a classic Triumph Stag that used to belong to her – and her legacy to me was the impetus to get my driving licence.

The Stag represented her mother, because she had driven the same car. It wasn't the original one because someone stole her mother's car, and she was heartbroken because it was the last remaining possession that she had of her mother, who had died when Amber was very young. It was ancient and riddled with rust, but it meant the world to her so, when the police couldn't find it, she put ads in the papers saying, 'Someone has stolen my mum's Stag. I don't care how much I pay to get it back. I just want it back.' Nothing.

It was a shame, but she found one that was almost identical, same model and year, so she bought that to replace it, and to continue the memory of her mum, whose loss she had always felt so keenly.

Whenever we got together for a Sunday roast with her family, my adopted family, she would say, 'I never had the luxury of having a mother when I was growing up.' She never imagined she would go the same way, because she had regular scans from the age of eighteen, but she had wanted a big family and, because she started having babies late, at thirty-seven, she was constantly in birth mode, for four years, which masked the symptoms. She was a wonderful mum and adored motherhood, so she was planning six or seven kids.

One day, soon after the funeral, I was walking past their house, which is not far from mine, and the Stag was parked out the front with a 'For Sale' sign on it. It hadn't been used in six years, because you can't put child seats in it.

The Stag hadn't been driven since Amber had Monty, back in October 2006, the year after my split with long-term partner Lloyd. I had rented my house out in the wake of our bust up and I was staying at her place, in her basement. I was in the middle of *Strictly Come Dancing* and she was heavily pregnant with Monty.

I came home after work one night and Amber was in labour. It was my sister Melanie's birthday, so I had to phone her before midnight; so, while Amber was screaming 'Aaaaargh' every few minutes, I was ringing Mel in Australia, and she asked me, 'What's all that noise in the background?'

'Don't worry,' I said. 'It's just Amber, she's in the middle of labour, she's having contractions, she's about to go to the hospital.'

When I got off the phone, I got my video camcorder out and started interviewing her. I had a spotlight on the camera and she was saying, 'The light's too bright ... turn them off!'

'I need the light,' I explained, but she was yelling, 'Stop filming me.'

'Amber, I want to record this for posterity,' I said, laughing. She was crouched over the sofa, which we called the slug zone, because that's where we liked to veg out and scoff Baileys and ice-cream – Bailey floaters – or just ice-cream while she was pregnant.

She and Mark were timing the contractions and when they were three minutes apart, she said, 'Oh, God, we've got to go, we've got to go NOW!' They used the Stag to get to the hospital and I filmed them clambering in. Amber, huge with child and screaming with pain, trying to climb into the passenger seat of the Stag was the most hilarious thing I've ever seen in my life. She was rushing around shouting, 'It's coming, it's coming, the baby's coming,' and screeching as Mark backed the car out, then they disappeared down the road, with Amber's screams trailing behind, which were louder than the rumble of the Stag's V8 engine.

A day or two later, she came back with a baby boy called Monty Revel, who she named after me.

After that, the Stag sat in the front of their garden until

she died, filling up with water, rusting. And, when I saw the 'For Sale', sign all those memories came flooding back. I knocked on the door, and Mark opened it.

'You're not selling that Stag?' I said.

'I have to,' he told me.

'Why?' I asked.

'Because I've got to buy Amber's headstone and I haven't got the money,' he explained. Poor Mark. There was only one thing I could do.

'Well, I'll buy it.' I said. 'You can't let it out of the family,'

'You haven't got a driving licence.' He pointed out, perfectly reasonably.

'Yes, I know,' I replied. 'But that's something I'll have to deal with. I've never owned a car, I've never got a licence, I don't know what to do about it, but I'll buy it. How much do you want for it?'

We didn't look at the value of the car. Instead, we went up to the funeral director to find out how much the headstone was going to cost and I gave him £3,500 for it.

By coincidence, our close mutual friend, Christopher Woods – known as Master Woods – went past a little later and thought he would do the same thing, even though he hadn't got his licence either, but I had beaten him to it.

I used to love this little car but it was when I bought the Triumph Stag that I knew it was time to learn how to drive ...

Because I hadn't passed my test, and the car was in no fit state for driving lessons, I had no alternative but to put it in for restoration. Thankfully, it took a year for Mark and Jerry from Enginuity, the Stag specialists, to restore it back to its former glory, because I had to have a bare metal re-spray, and a lot more work, which gave me time to learn to drive. The downside was that it ended up costing £35,000!

It was a ridiculous amount of money. I thought, when I bought it, I would spend fifteen thousand on it to tart it up, but then another ten went on and then I kept getting calls saying, 'You need this part' or 'Something else has broken down', so in the end it was a fortune. But it was a labour of love, and I was happy just to have the car and it gave me the motivation to get my driving licence.

I looked in my diary for that year and I thought, 'Right, I have seven weeks where I'm in London and I can do an intensive course of driving lessons.' Series nine of *Strictly* was just starting so I knew I was going be in London and I booked lesson between 11 a.m. and 1 p.m. every single day, except weekends, until 23 November, when I could take the test. After that, I had to go away so, if I failed, there wasn't going to be another opportunity to do it again until the May of the following year; therefore, it was imperative that I passed my test, no matter what. I studied and studied, and did three weeks of practical driving while I was studying the handbook. I passed my hazard perception test and the written test – with flying colours – and then I had three weeks until the test, so I drove every day in our two-hour lessons. And my driving instructor, Simon Michaelson, was brilliant and very funny scoring me marks out of ten for all my maneouvres.

It was great fun, and I thoroughly enjoyed it, but there were however, a whole host of near misses during those lessons. I drove up over the kerbs on several occasions; turning left, I nearly had an accident with a bus because I didn't see it – I had to do an emergency stop at a roundabout because I was pulling out and the bus was driving straight at me; I had to go up on the kerb at fifty miles an hour because I hadn't slowed down enough for a single-lane bridge. I was very good at parking, though.

To my relief, I passed the test first time and, at the age of forty-six, I could finally get behind a wheel.

The first time I drove to the BBC and parked in their multi-storey car park, I got in a total panic. When I went to leave, I couldn't get out of the car park! I assumed you would go down to the ground floor to drive out, but oh, no, not at the Beeb. I was driving round and round, running into dead ends and I could not find an exit. Eventually, I found an attendant.

'I may be stupid, but how do I get out of this car park?' I asked rather sheepishly. He said, 'You go up to the top floor and then there's a spiral down.'

So you have to go up six storeys in order to drive back

down to the ground. No wonder I couldn't work it out.

After passing my test, I still had a six-month wait until the Stag was ready, and I finally picked it up in the summer of 2012. Mark and Jerry had done a sterling job with the restoration! 'Ralf', Amber and my name for the car, named after her dearly departed pet dog, was stunning, sexy and brand new.

As soon as I drove it away from the workshop, looking all shiny, new and gorgeous, I had a lesson with my instructor because I had learned in a manual and the Stag is automatic. I also wanted to have a lesson on driving on the motorway, as I hadn't done that before. The very next day, I embarked on my first road trip, and took my friend Alex Murphy, a lighting technician I met on the *Strictly Come Dancing Live* tour, along for the ride. We drove all round Cornwall, a total of 1,500 miles in the glorious sunshine with the top down, and I loved it. We had a ball. We pretended we were Thelma and Louise, donning outrageous wigs, head scarfs and sunglasses just to freak people out in all the little villages we were driving through. It was a great laugh stopping and taking photos at random signs dressed as the famous duo. The only thing missing was Brad Pitt – not that there was much room in the back of the Stag for that part of the story to happen. Amber would have been thrilled to see her beloved 'Ralf' on such a fun-filled journey.

The summer before I got my licence, I embarked on a very different car journey when the BBC invited me to appear on *Celebrity Antiques Road Trip*.

'That sounds like fun,' I said. 'Who am I on with?'

'Ann Widdecombe,' came the reply. 'You're battling against each other to see who can make the most profit at auction.'

We were filming on a boiling hot day in July 2011 and, when I arrived at some ungodly hour of the morning, Ann greeted me with a cheery, 'Hello!' Then she said, 'Here we are. Back together again.'

I said, 'We're like Laurel and Hardy, you and I, darling – inseparable!'

As well as dancing on tour, we had already appeared together on the quiz show *Pointless*, where we were a complete disaster, embarrassingly bad, and were first out. But we had a laugh and raised money for charity so that was fine, and the *Antiques Road Trip* was a blast.

The idea is that you drive around the country looking for antique bargains and then see who does best at auction. We started in the same car together, and I only had my L plates so I wasn't allowed to drive, except on private property, so Ann was supposed to drive. We had to be in classic cars, but the problem with Ann and vintage motors is that she can't reach the pedals – at all! Getting her in and out of the car was a challenge and then, the first time we actually got her in, she said, 'I can't reach the pedals.'

The production team put cushions on the seats to try to get her as close as possible – her boobs were literally on the steering wheel and her feet were still swinging about trying to reach the pedals. By this time, we were all doubled over in hysterical laughter.

To add to our predicament, these old-fashioned cars had bench seats at the front. The engineers decided to try to push the seat forward, and then I became the problem, because I'm 6'2", so when Ann could finally touch the pedals, I was sitting bolt upright with my knees around my chin. It was the funniest thing I think I've ever done in my life.

It was a peculiar old car, an Austin A40 sports convertible built in 1950, and, because of the way it was painted in orange and cream, it looked like a little ice-cream van. The engine was started by pulling a lever out, then there was the old-fashioned column gear shift, which is on the steering wheel, and Ann couldn't get it into gear. They told her, 'Just drive slowly down there, and then stop,' and then someone had to stop the engine for her, and I was trying to operate the gears while she was pushing the clutch in. It was like a nightmare, the blind leading the blind.

After struggling with that, she refused to drive it because she said it wasn't roadworthy, and she was acting like the most dangerous thing she had ever had to do was drive down this little lane. We were going about five miles an hour down the lane, then, when they were trying to reverse it, it kept stalling. Everything that could go wrong with it went wrong.

We did a couple of exit and arrival shots, trying not to giggle and trying to look natural, because we were all miked up and there was a car in front of us, filming, as we drove along having a chat. We had to do a lot of adlibbing about how I was going to beat her and how she was going to beat me and then, when that was done, we were separated so we could go off with our antiques expert.

Ann was with Mark Stacey and I was with Catherine Southon. I think poor Mark was a nervous wreck, because he didn't know what Ann was going to be like, and he thought that he'd get me because we're both camp queens. I could see us shopping for antiques together, but I got Catherine, who was fabulous.

It one of those beautiful summer mornings and, while they were sorting out what they were going to do about the car – because Ann was refusing to drive it and I couldn't legally drive, which made the road trip part of the show pretty difficult – Ann and I sat on a bench in the middle of the countryside looking at the cows. She was identifying the different breeds to me, which was all quite interesting but totally surreal.

In the end, Mark said that he would drive it and we got ready to leave. We all had to set off at different times, and we were to travel to various places and shop for some treasures, but separately, so we weren't allowed to see each other or meet each other along the way. Our patch was Devon and Somerset, which is Ann's neck of the woods, but it was a completely unfamiliar part of the world as far as I was concerned.

I went off in my car, a lovely old Triumph, with Catherine at the wheel, and Ann went off on her merry way with Mark. We didn't see Ann again and, after a while, I thought, 'We haven't heard from them at all. That's really weird.' Although we are not supposed to meet, they should have been beating us to some of the stores, but there was no sign of her. Then their production crew radioed to say the car had broken down and that Mark and Ann were sitting in searing heat in a country lane for four hours. They had pulled the starter and the whole lever came out, leaving a mess of wires dangling down, and they were stuck, losing valuable shopping time.

Catherine and I didn't fare much better in our car. We were going up a hill and Catherine put the handbrake on,

GRANVILLE BOYS'
HIGH SCHOOL
1978
RECORDER CONSORT

*bove (centre front):* I was always full of hot air! Not sure
*ave* Arch will be calling upon my services any time soon.

*Left:* The many faces of CRH,
seen here in full make-up with
my sister Melanie.

Mean and moody in the 1980s – little has changed!

*ove and right*: Make-up and corsets are a man's best
*end* … but my bark has always been worse than my bite!

*elow*: Getting a helping hand from Vincent to go live.

Couldn't fit 'seven' pictures of Head Judge Len Goodman on the
page so these will have to suffice.

*Above*: And it's a perfect 10 from the *Strictly* Judges (© BBC).

*Below*: Tess Daly always looking fab-u-lous!

Zoë Ball

Natalie Cassidy

Michael Vaughn

Harry Judd

ott Maslen

Nancy Dell'Olio

'ith over 100 celebrity dancers across all the series
; tricky to pick a favourite!

*Above*: Flying high with my fabulous family: Gail (Grant's mum), Grant, Beverley (my mum), and Sue (my sister).

*Left*: Sharing a pint with my manager and friend Gavin Barker

but the handbrake fell off in her hand. We had no handbrake, so she had to try to ride the clutch for the whole journey.

Then it conked out, on a hill, but as there was no handbrake she had to have her foot on the brake the entire time. We were in the middle of the road and, when an engineer turned up, she had to try to get her foot off the brake as he slid his foot on it. I got out and was holding the car from behind to stop it going backwards, and Catherine's trying to manoeuvre herself up and over the bloody door while the engineer is putting his foot on the brake, and trying to get in and start the bloody thing.

We walked up this enormous hill, in the blazing heat, and then waited at the top until they could get the car going again, and Catherine had to drive it without the handbrake for the rest of the day.

When it came to the auction day, which was weeks after we'd bought our items, I'd chosen this big wooden box for a huge amount of money, thinking I was going to make a killing on it. It was a bit like a tool box, but it was mahogany and just beautiful. We spent £260 on it, and we only had a budget of £400, but I thought it was worth going for anyway. We got to the auction and my item was the first thing up, and there was only one bid, for £200, so that's what it went for. So that was the first nail in my coffin. Ann had bought the most ridiculous tea set and that made money – which I found incredible – but she ended up winning.

But there wasn't just the auction to film that day. We were back in the same old car and we had to do another shot of Ann driving into a car park – with me in the passenger seat. I was trying not to laugh because she was muttering under her breath the whole time, saying, 'There's no way I'm doing that', and 'I won't be held responsible.' It sounded a bit like a celebrity 'Don't they know I'm a star' rant, but she was only worried about the health and safety.

In the end, they got the shot, but we were puttering along at about two miles an hour, so they must have had to speed the footage up. The whole episode was hilarious.

# CHAPTER 5

# THE BODY BEAUTIFUL

When I was growing up in Ballarat, near Melbourne, I was bullied at school for being fat. The local kids used to call me 'Tits' because, even as a child, I had man boobs. In my teens, I took up dancing and, simultaneously, became anorexic, so I was all skin and bones, but I still had fat boobs. No matter how skinny or fit I was, I couldn't shift the unsightly bulk around my chest.

Because of my cruel nickname at school, the last thing I wanted was tits, but they never went away. There were times when I had the body beautiful, like when I danced at the Lido in Paris, and I was on the lowest fat, lowest carb,

lowest everything diet and trying to work out every day to build up muscle. Even then, the flesh around my nipples looked big and horrible and blubby and I hated it. For me to get my chest down to a normal size, I would have to be extremely thin, and that looks ugly, because my ribs stuck out. So I've always had a battle with my weight and being a dancer makes you incredibly body conscious because you are surrounded by mirrors and being constantly judged on your looks as well as your talent.

Many years after I gave up dance, I discovered that my problem was actually a medical condition called gynecomastia, where benign breast tissue builds up underneath the nipple in a man and, no matter how much you diet, no matter how much you exercise, it won't shift. After all those years of fruitless attempts, I was told it wasn't fat, it was breast tissue.

A few years ago, I had put on weight while working on *Strictly* and my big old boobies were driving me nuts. I was really self-conscious about them and I was sick of them bouncing up and down because it felt uncomfortable. I decided to look into what could be done. So I booked a consultation with a surgeon in Harley Street and he said, 'Yes, we can do this.'

'You're not going to look like a twenty-year-old,' he warned. As if! 'But you will have a flat chest.'

'That is all I want,' I said.

The doctor also looked at the fat deposits on my back and said, 'I can make that look better because you're very broad of hip.' So he said he could trim that down, and that meant the fat wouldn't go there any more.

It was £3,500 for the pecs and the same again for my back fat. I realize how lucky I am, because I have enough money to go and pay for a good surgeon. This is not an operation you can have on the NHS because it's not life or death, its aesthetic, so they see it as cosmetic, but it can be horrible to live with and can ruin your confidence. In extreme cases, it could have a massive impact on someone's life.

It's incredible how it changes the lives of men, because people think that women are body conscious, but men, if they've got gynecomastia or just man boobs – moobs as they call them – it's embarrassing. Men are supposed to have pecs, not moobs and it is awful. You can never take your shirt off in the sun, you're always worried about someone touching you, or getting undressed in front of a new partner, and it's horrific.

As I got older, I have tried to get less and less bothered by it. When I turned forty, I tried telling myself, 'Look, Craig, you don't need to impress anyone, you don't need to be like ripped and body beautiful. Your creative mind is your best asset and that's all you need.' But being on television makes you look at yourself harder than you would necessarily in real life and you worry about other people's impressions of you. Plus, of course, as you get older it gets worse, because they get bigger and droop.

In May 2011, I went in for the operation, which was two hours long. The fat removal involved them inserting an iron rod through a hole in the side of your pecs and hoovering the stuff out and for the gynecomastia, they cut around the nipple and then snip out the breast tissue and then fit the nipple back.

For the back fat, again, they go in from the side and use the high-powered hoover and they told me afterwards I was a tough job, because there was so much back fat! I had no idea how much extra padding I had around my hips. They took a litre of fat and tissue out of each breast and four litres in total.

Grant, who worked in Harley Street, was there when I came round from the op and was able to take me home.

Initially, the pain was excruciating and for a few days afterwards I felt like I'd been punched in the chest, about five hundred times, or done a major massive workout and *really* overdone it to the point of doing damage. As I was swathed in bandages, I also started to panic about the end result, what it would look like and whether there would be scarring.

Once the bandages were off, however, I looked at my chest in the mirror and I just broke down in tears. It was a complete success, but I was overcome with a mixture of relief, joy and regret for all the wasted years. My first thought was, 'Why didn't I have this done ages ago?' It was worth every single penny I had paid for it. Even if I hadn't been in a well-paid job, knowing what I do now, I would have saved up my whole life to have it done. I felt wonderful.

As an added bonus, the operation also spurred me into getting fit again and losing weight. When you have a major operation like that, which prevents the fat going to certain parts of the body, it will go elsewhere, so you have to be very careful about what you do and what you eat and the surgeon put me on a strict regime to keep me trim. I had to lose ten kilos before I even had the operation so I had already dieted for three months.

I also knew I would have to do some serious exercise. I had expected to see the muscle that had been lurking behind the fat and the breast tissue but there didn't seem to be that much and, in fact, I looked like a pre-pubescent boy. I would have to do some strength and endurance training on my chest, and rebuild my pecs from scratch. But there was absolutely no visable scarring, and I was really chuffed.

Although I had fat removed from the hips, I stopped short of having my tummy done because I was scared. I had heard terrible stories about blood filling up the scrotum and I'd seen images of bad tummy ops, that leave horrible scarring. All I really cared about was my chest because it had been the bane of my life.

After the op, I ended up having a flat chest and a bit of a pot belly, which I loved because I looked like a normal bloke, rather than having these saggy, baggy elephant tits. For me it was a dramatic change. For people at home watching the telly it might not even be noticeable, because I have always been able to hide it under suits.

The immediate aftermath of the operation proved a bit of a nightmare. You have to wear compression body suits that are really, really tight and squeeze everything, except your bits and pieces, every single day for two months. If the body isn't compressed, the skin becomes loose and looks like an eighty-year-old's. So I wore those in public all the time, and had to wear high-necked tops to hide them. To make matters worse, it was summer and the suits were stifling in the heat.

I even wore one to Buckingham Palace to meet Camilla, the Duchess of Cornwall, and Dame Shirley Bassey. I was invited to a garden party where Camilla was due to make a speech and I had to respond to her and, afterwards, we chatted to Shirley Bassey. I was aware of the compression suit all the time, and I was boiling hot, but obviously I didn't want anyone to know. I certainly wasn't going to say, 'Oi, Shirley, guess what? I've just had my tits done!'

I didn't tell Camilla about it either, even though we are quite good friends and she is a wonderful woman. It seems vain, and I suppose it is, but I'm in an industry that is very body conscious and I'm getting old so it had sapped my confidence.

Vain or not, it was the best seven grand I've ever spent. Ever!

On the subject of 'getting work done', I have often been accused of having botox treatments or facelifts. I personally think men look better without all of that stuff. You only need to look at Barry Manilow to know that it's wrong for men to have surgery.

I have never had botox injections but people think I have, perhaps because I've learned how to relax my facial muscles and I tend to keep my face deadpan for delivery on the show. I can't imagine trying to express myself with a plastic face.

When I need to express myself, I raise my left eyebrow a lot, and if I couldn't do that, I don't know how my character would come across. No one wants to be that botoxed, 'ripped up and sewn together' Frankenstein. No one wants to look like Donatella Versace, darling!

Soon after the op, I travelled to America to film *Scream Extreme*, with Bruno Tonioli and Duncan James from Blue. It's a crazy quiz show in which has celebrities answer questions while riding the most horrific rollercoasters, and each point you earn means cash for the member of the public playing with you. It was filmed in Los Angeles, at Six Flags Magic Mountain, which has some of the fastest, highest and scariest rides in the world. It was also in searing heat, and I was still wearing a compression suit underneath my clothes, which was horribly uncomfortable, but it was great fun.

They closed all the rides down for the normal punters briefly, so only the contestants and the crew were allowed on them – and it was really scary. I had a camera on a meter-long rod strapped to my chest to capture my terrified reactions, and we were 150 feet in the air, just dangling.

I've always been petrified of heights and that's why I jumped out of an aeroplane five years ago back in Queenstown, New Zealand, to try to get over the fear. Skydiving from 15,000 feet over Queenstown seemed to do the trick and make me a little less afraid, which came in handy when they 'parachuted' me and Bruno into Wembley arena in the last series of *Strictly*. I was really calm as we dangled in the harness, above the huge arena, and even managed to take some pictures from up there. But poor Bruno was terrified. His face was a picture.

Even though I'm better with heights these days, I'm not a fan of rollercoasters but, because I was answering loads of questions at the same time, it was less terrifying for some reason. I was up against Bruno and it was the UK versus America, so I had a British girl as my partner and he had an American man. At one point, I had to do animal noises so my partner could identify them, and that wasn't easy as we're racing down a track at 150 feet.

It was a brilliant thing to do, because I got to go on the highest, most sensational rides in the world, and the scariest ones, and I was fast tracked through each one of them. I didn't have to queue – and that's what I loved about it the most actually. But Bruno never stopped swearing! They had to bleep most of what he said out of the programme and, at one point, he asked. 'Why did I do this? Why did I take this job?'

'Money, darling?' I said.

Actually, the whole thing was really good fun because they filmed the shows in a block, so back at the hotel we hung out with the other competing celebrities. There was actress Sheridan Smith, who was great company, Sam Faiers and Coolio. Duncan was the host of the show and he is a lovely, genuine guy, really adorable. Grant came with me on that trip – we went on to San Francisco for a holiday – and it was really beautiful weather, blazing sunshine.

Plus, I beat Bruno, which added to my enjoyment of the day!

## CHAPTER 6

# GOD SAVE THE QUEEN

My road to British citizenship began in 1989, when I first moved to London, at the age of twenty-four. My previous experience of the UK had been a flying visit on a sightseeing tour when I was seventeen. My lasting impression of that first trip was that it was really hot and sultry in September, which I wasn't expecting, and because I thought in terms of dollars I thought everything was really cheap. A cassette was 99p, which translated in my head to 99 cents, so I thought my money was going much further than it was,

I still hadn't learned my financial lesson the first time I came for more than a visit. It was April Fool's Day 1989 when I arrived at Heathrow and jumped straight into in a taxi. I was the fool – it cost me £60! At that time, I had been living in Paris for a year and was used to French francs. I had 10,000 francs, which equated to £1,000 so £60 for a cab was a lot of money, and as I paid, I was thinking, 'Oh, no, dis-ah-ster. This isn't going to last long'. By the time I'd stumped up a month's rent and a month in advance, there wasn't a lot of change out of a grand. Time to wait tables.

On the subject of money, it took me a while to get used to British notes because they were huge. The £50 and £20 notes seemed so big that they wouldn't fit in my wallet and the colours were dull, dull, dull. Australian notes are all different colours and much smaller, and here I was with a £50 the size of a sheet of A3 paper – absolutely enormous!

Another aspect that didn't help my debt management was that everyone here paid by cheque. If you went to the off-licence or the grocer's, you could just write a cheque, and all you needed was a cheque guarantee card. I couldn't believe it. In Australia, we've had bank cards for ever, and you only used cheques to send through the post. You can't just write one in a store.

In my living room, to this day, is a beautiful African sable antelope's head named Anthula, who serves as a constant reminder of my frivolous youthful spending. I saw her in Camden market and couldn't resist – despite a price tag of

£160. I was broke, and I couldn't afford it, and that was a great deal of money twenty years ago but I had to have it. And I had cheques. The guarantee card only went up to £50 so I wrote three cheques for £50 and one for £10. It was highly dangerous for me because I'd never before been able to walk into a shop and pay for something so expensive, even if I didn't have the money in the account. You could even walk into some shops and cash a cheque. I remember going on a trip to Paris once and I just cashed four cheques for £50 each for spending money. I couldn't believe they would let me do it. And that's how I got into debt. I ended up in £800 deficit – purely because of my chequebook. I used them everywhere. In one shop, I even wrote a cheque for 30p!

When I arrived everything was in pounds and ounces, which was pretty confusing. I was schooled in the metric system and I had no idea what half a pound of mince was, or a pound of apples. Trying to think in miles instead of kilometres was totally bizarre, because I would think 'I can walk that, it's only three …' but it would be three miles instead of three kilometres, which meant I arrived everywhere late, with aching feet. It's those stupid little things that throw you because you've had one life, where you're used to a metric system and then a whole new world where you're supposed to know feet, inches and yards. I still don't know what a yard is. In a car, when the speedometer said it was doing 70, I would think that was dead slow. I had to keep reminding myself that was over 110 km/h. I got my provisional licence when I first got here and I was driving around London with L plates on, with any willing licence holder I could find in the passenger seat.

Driving is another oddity and particularly the fact that you can park on the wrong side of the road – you can be driving in one direction and then cross the street to park. That was weird to me. In Australia, if you see a parking space on the other side you have to go down the street, turn around and then come back to it, so that all the cars face the same way.

Pints were an alien concept too. Everyone drinks out of small glasses in Australia because the beer gets warm, and here you have warm beer, deliberately. I found that disgusting back then and it's something I still can't get used to. A beer has got to be ice, ice cold and here it's pumped out flat and warm – eugh! And the pints were huge. I remember holding my first one and thinking, 'This is enormous. How on earth am I going to drink that?' The pub culture is totally different as well because the pubs are really small, dark and oaky, and you hit your head on the racks of glasses, nothing like the modern pubs at home.

Coming from an English-speaking country is an obvious

advantage when moving to the UK, but it doesn't entirely breach the language barrier. There were so many different accents in London alone, and I could never understand taxi drivers because they talk a million miles an hour. I didn't catch a word. My first theatre job in Britain was a touring production with Danny La Rue and the regional accents were unbelievable. There were some Northern accents that I just couldn't understand. I was constantly asking, 'I'm sorry, can you say that again?' Then I went to Scotland for the first time – not a hope! I couldn't even order a drink. I couldn't understand what was being said at all – it sounded like a foreign language.

London is incredibly multi-cultural and that's what I adore about it, it's fantastic. I had never seen so many different coloured faces in my life as I did in London. I was amazed when I got the tube for the first time. I don't know what I was expecting, but I suppose I imagined Britain was mostly white. In Australia, the ethnic minority is small; in London it's huge! But what I noticed was that they all had posh accents. It is quite arresting if you're not used to it and everyone I know who has come over from Australia has remarked on it.

The city is also incredibly densely populated compared to Melbourne, the nearest city when I was growing up. When you consider there are only twenty-two million people in the whole of Australia and there are nearly ten million in London alone, in just one city. Sydney and Melbourne have about four million, so London is really busy but I love the hustle and bustle of the place. Even so, using the tube for the first time was just frightening. I was scared to death of it. All those things were really quite weird – getting a travel card, working out what zone you are going to, where to change lines. I was used to buying tickets on trams, which is a lot simpler. I had a prequel to it, in Paris, because I used the Metro frequently, but the London Underground is something else.

Up on the street, my nose became a casualty of all the exhaust fumes. When I blew my nose, the black gunge that came out was disgusting. If you've had fresh air all your life and you come here, your nose doesn't process all the chemicals and exhaust fumes in the air, so when you blow your nose it's black, which is really quite alarming. Buses are a lot more eco-friendly now but in those days the streets were full of the old Routemaster buses and they would belch black fumes into the air. And everyone was smoking on the top deck. I couldn't believe you were allowed to smoke on a bus. The night buses were awful. I used to catch the N29 and it was rough as anything, with all the smokers upstairs sitting in a toxic smog. Australia was completely ahead of its time in that respect and they haven't allowed smoking in public places for decades. Even in Paris, where you could smoke in cafés, it was totally new to me. But in London, you were even allowed to smoke on tubes until the eighties, and it wasn't fully banned in the station until the King's Cross fire in 1987.

As a wide-eyed youth arriving in the UK, it felt a little like living in a movie. The afternoon teas, the cucumber sandwiches, the champagne and the strawberries and cream at Wimbledon were all things we'd seen in British movies and to find out it was real was the most bizarre thing. Even more mind-blowing was seeing Pall Mall, Leicester Square and Euston – all places from the Monopoly Board. I'd been playing that game all my life and I wandered around saying, 'Oh, my God! It's Piccadilly Circus, it's Trafalgar Square!' You know all the names but you never associate anything with them until you see them for real. I would also discover streets, counties and towns and think, 'Oh, that's an Australian name.' All the place names in Australia, like Surrey and Brighton, come from here but it doesn't occur to you while you are living there because they are just local names. When you're fresh off the boat in the UK you suddenly think, 'Wow, this is where it all started.' You feel a bit like you're coming home. I felt immediately comfortable in the place.

These days, I am so used to London, where no one looks

into each other's eyes, no one acknowledges you, that I find aspects of Australia a bit odd. Back home, everyone says, 'G'day, mate, how's it going?' when you're walking along the street and I now find that a bit scary, like they want to stab me or rob me, when they're just being friendly. London is full of busy people going about their business and not even looking at each other. But I like that, probably because I am more of a city boy and have been all my life. I enjoy the anonymity of it all. Of course, I don't have that any more but then I came to London to seek fame and fortune, so I'm not complaining.

On 20 August 2011, this boy from Oz finally became a British citizen. And it was about time. I'd been living and working in the UK for twenty-two years, half my life, and had been meaning to become a fully-fledged Brit for ages. I love living in London and, although my family are still in Australia, Britain has become my home.

Apart from my passion for all things British, there was a practical reason for my interest in citizenship. Queues. No, not the Brits' legendary love for them, but my own passionate hatred for standing in them at airports. The final straw came at Heathrow, in May 2009, when I returned home after eight weeks in New Zealand and a break in Australia.

I had just finished my first season of *Dancing With the Stars* and after we wrapped I flew to Melbourne, then had a holiday in Broome, Western Australia, with my sister, Sue – where I got an ear infection so they had to leave me there because I couldn't fly. Then I flew to Perth, then Ballarat, back to Auckland and finally back to the UK. After a long and tiring flight, I got to immigration to find that about five planes had just landed from India, China and all over the place – the queue must have been about two hours long. In my exhausted and frustrated state, I watched the UK citizens flashing their passports and waltzing through and I thought, 'This is pathetic. I really should apply for my British passport.' It would be *so* much easier to get about.

My job, especially my theatre work, means I travel *a lot*. And, despite being granted Indefinite Leave to Remain (ILR), I still had to fill out a pile of paperwork every time I returned and then join a queue – which was always approximately a million people long. It was ridiculous – and brought about by my own laziness. At that moment, as I ached to get home to my own bed, I knew I had to pull my finger out and give it a go.

One of the reasons I had put it off is that, until 2002, anyone applying for citizenship of another country automatically lost their Australian passport. That meant I would have needed a holiday visa to go home and visit my family in Melbourne, which was absurd. My family is really, really important to me so I couldn't have that.

Coincidentally, my friend Rebecca Hobbs, who was a contestant on *Dancing With the Stars*, had just applied for British Citizenship after four years and got it, and she invited me to her ceremony. And that really spurred me on. I asked her if it was very hard, and she said, 'The book's a bit tricky. There's a lot of queuing, the test centre is a bit of a nightmare ...' But, to hell with it, if she could do it, so could I. I mean I'd been living in the UK for twenty-two years! I had the books at home anyway, because I had bought them years before, skimmed through them, thought it all looked a bit too much, and never looked at them again. Then, in April 2010, when Grant and I were off to the Maldives for two weeks, I decided to take them with me. The plan was to relax for two weeks and do nothing, but I spent a fortnight in the glorious sunshine quietly doing citizenship tests and poor Grant spent the whole time asking me questions out of the book. It must have ruined his holiday, but still ... I would recommend it as a fabulous place to swot up.

The facts you have to learn for the test are mind-boggling! The percentage of the population living in step-families, the percentage of ethnic minorities in Scotland and the Muslim population of Northern Ireland were among the trickier questions. The funny thing about this is that it's all based on the 2001 census and when you're learning it, you also learn the updated population, so you have to remember two different sets of figures. Then they try to throw you by expressing percentages as decimals, so the question could be:

What was the approximate percentage of people in the UK in 2001 who said they were Muslims?

a) 0.017

b) 0.019

c) 0.027

d) 0.037

The answer is actually 2.7%, which is C, so they try to trick you with this bizarre decimal point as well. It's bonkers.

Anyway, I booked the test, paid my £34, and was allocated a test date a month later, in Islington. The test is done in packs of thirty people at a time, in a room where there are rows and rows of computers. You have forty-five minutes to answer twenty-four questions.

The test centre felt a bit like being back at school, like we'd all been naughty children and we were being put in detention. Everyone queues up, all different shapes and sizes, and skin colours, obviously, but we were all people after one thing – British Citizenship. (By the way, I might have British citizenship but I still can't say it! Try saying it fast – it's a real tongue twister.)

When I arrived at the test centre, I had to hand in my passport, which they take as proof of identity and country of origin. As I stood in the queue, the official took my passport and without opening it said, rather loudly, 'Oh, we know who you are, Craig Revel Horwood.' That piled the pressure on because people started recognizing me, and all I was thinking was, 'This is hideous! What if I fail? It would be public disgrace!' Even as we waited for the test to begin, I signed five autographs for my fellow immigrants. The more people that recognized me the more panic-stricken I got. I was telling myself, 'I've got to pass. I've been living in this country for twenty-two years, I work on BBC1, and it would be so horrendous if I fail. Imagine the shame.'

Amazing as it may seem, I have never sat a proper big written exam in my life. I didn't finish school so I've never done any kind of exam before. By this time I hadn't even taken my driving test. So, as you can imagine, I was an absolute nervous wreck.

As usual, I was trying to cover it up with bravado and jokes, and 'Oh, dahlings!' But no amount of 'dahlings' are going to help you pass! You have to know what you're doing. Plus, I didn't want to take a ridiculously long time, I wanted to look efficient and romp through it. So I swotted up like a demon, ploughing through hundreds of mock tests on the computer at home, just so I could do it without thinking, knowing every single question, and every single answer. I was a maniac with it. I was doing tests in the backs of cars and taxis; at home, I wasn't watching television or reading the paper – every spare moment I was clicking buttons and when one test finished I started another one. The day before the exam, I must have done thirty mocks, just to make sure I felt confident enough to get in the car and actually arrive at the test centre.

On the day, everyone was very nice, explaining where you have to go and what you have to do. You get a fifteen-minute briefing about what you can and can't do, then you go in and place you passport in front of you on the desk, on the right hand side, next to the computer mouse. Then they give you a practice run to get you used to the computer system, and you click when you want the test to begin. After that, there's no going back. If your phone rings, you are instantly disqualified and talking is strictly forbidden. There are officials walking up and down the aisles and staring at you, and it's all deathly silent. It's *really scary*. But when the test got underway, my hard work paid off. I knew the answers to all of the questions and I literally finished in four minutes!

After the test, I had to wait in another queue for my

interview, which takes place before you get your test results and is horrendously nerve-wracking. After what seemed an eternity, I was called into the office and an official asked me a few questions, tapping away on his computer impassively, then he handed over my results. A pass. *Fantastic.*

But that wasn't the end of it. I joined yet another queue to get yet another certificate, which is signed to say you've passed. By now, I'd compiled a huge great dossier of paperwork, so that I could finally apply for full British citizenship, and I also had to list every single moment I'd spent out of the country in the last seven years and, in my line of work, that's a hell of a lot of travel. I have been working all over Europe, as well as spending weeks in New Zealand, and I'm backwards and forwards all the time. It took me two weeks to put together a list of all my wanderings.

When all that was done, I had to wait a month while they checked over the papers and then I went through a checking agency at the council, which costs another £50. I waited in a little room, nervously chewing my nails, before being invited in and told I was missing one vital piece of paper, and had to go away and come back again, so I had to book another appointment. It was so frustrating. When all the paperwork was finally put though, and the application submitted, they said, 'Thank you very much. We'll let you know. It could take anything between three months and six months.' I was horrified – that was three to six months without my passport. Dis-ah-ster!

There was nothing more I could do. I waited and waited and waited. Then one afternoon I was in a car going to the BBC, the phone rang and a voice said, 'Hello, is that Mr Craig Revel Horwood?'

'Yes', I answered.

'Hello', said the voice. 'I'm from the UK Border Agency and I'd like to talk to you about your application to become a British citizen'. My heart sank. I couldn't understand why they were ringing me because I was told to expect a letter, so I feared the worst. But to my relief he said, 'We've been discussing your case this morning, and we have decided to welcome you to Britain.'

I yelped, 'Hurrah!!!' I loved it. I was finally going to be a British citizen. I'm not sure everyone gets the personal phone call. I thought it was rather odd and I'm sure they were having a good old laugh at my horrendous passport photos back in the office.

The citizenship ceremony was brilliant, full of pomp and circumstance, which I love! We hired the biggest room at Camden Town Hall, which seats 180 guests, but I decided to keep it small, at around sixty. It's a beautiful chamber, like an old courtroom with dark wood panels and circular benches. On the back wall, there were two big flags and a massive photo of the queen. It looked gorgeous. It felt very regal, very royal.

I was planning to wear a suit to the ceremony but, to mark the occasion, Grant and my friend David bought me some Union Jack epaulettes that were smothered in Swarovski crystals, and too heavy for the fabric. I needed something more heavy-duty and, the night before, in a mad rush, I found a red military style mess jacket in a hire shop round the corner. It was way too small for me but it was only one I could find that was red, so I wore it with the epaulettes and some Union Jack cufflinks.

On the day, I was slightly nervous because I didn't want to screw up the oath – which of course I did. The lady who was presiding over the ceremony welcomed everybody and then introduced me, and I chaînés turned into the seat. (This is a common abbreviation for *tours chaînés déboulés*, which is a series of quick 360-degree complete-rotation turns on alternating feet with progression, or chain, along a straight line or circle. The majority of the revolution is completed on the leading foot with the remainder on the trailing foot when it closes in first position. The turns are done with the feet in a small, tight first position releve. 'Spotting' of the head is used to stabilize the torso in this and all turning exercises in ballet. They are also known as 'chaînés tournes'. In classical ballet each rotation is done on pointes or demi-pointes, the balls of the feet. So now you know!) The lady went on to explain the proceedings and then gave a great long spiel about what Camden has to offer in the way of shopping! I've been living in Camden for twenty years, so it was quite bizarre to hear the tourist information speech – 'Camden has a lot of facilities to offer, including a beautiful shopping area and, of course, Camden Market is a popular place for tourists. You can get all sorts of wonderful things in Camden Market, from bric-a-brac to vintage clothes ...' It was the oddest thing.

Then I pledged my allegiance to the Queen, and I did it beautifully except that I stumbled over one word. I wanted to read it like a proper Brit, so I put on my poshest accent. Since moving here, I've lost my Aussie twang and it's now a really bastardized accent, which is obviously familiar to fans of *Strictly*. I tend to hang around posh people, like my best friend Christopher Woods, and I end up subconsciously copying them. Hence the drawn-out vowels, and the 'dahlings.'

Talking of posh, one of the highlights of the ceremony was reading out the lovely letter I received from Camilla, the Duchess of Cornwall, wishing me well. It read:

*Dear Craig,*

*There is nothing quite like a pom. I'm so sorry not to be with you on this very special day but it is wonderful news to hear that you are now one of us. With my best wishes to you, Camilla.*

*PS. I'm looking forward to seeing the next series of Strictly. I hope that we can come.*

The Duchess of Cornwall is the President and I am a patron of the National Osteoporosis Society. I know she's also a big fan of *Strictly*!

Nice to know even the royal family aren't too proud to blag a seat at *Strictly*.

Oath over, I did a run around the room, shaking hands and kissing people, then everyone put on masks of the royal family and I had my royal portrait. I hope I wasn't committing treason!

After the ceremony, we went across to St Pancras to the champagne-and-oyster bar, which had recently been refurbished and is gorgeous. We had a wonderful trumpeter, my good friend Karen Mann, playing 'Rule Britannia', while I danced on the table – naturally. Karen played Viv Nicholson in my production of *Spend Spend Spend* and her girlfriend is Sarah Travis, the musical director I work with in the theatre. Outside the station, I laid on a Routemaster, the traditional red double-decker bus, to take everyone back to my house – and it was chucking it down with rain. When I had left the house, it was looking glorious, the BBQ was out in the open, the party balloons were on the patio and I planned to use all the space I had outside. The rain was a complete disaster – but somehow fitting weather for my first day as a fully-fledged Brit. So all the guests splashed through the downpour onto the bus and, with rain lashing against the windows, struck up a chorus of 'Summer Holiday'. The old Routemaster was a little bit leaky too, so everyone arrived at the house dripping wet; and every inch of the house was soon crammed with damp people.

The party food was 'British meets Australian'. From down under, we had barbecue shapes – octagonal biscuits with flavour you can actually see – Coolmints, Fantails, Minties. From the UK, we had pork pies, cream-cheese-and-cucumber sandwiches, bangers and Union Jack cupcakes. I got so many Union Jack presents, my house now looks like the Buckingham Palace gift shop, with red, white and blue cushions, mugs and glasses everywhere.

Glorious sunshine did eventually win through on the day and the celebrations went from midday to midnight. It was *fab-u-lous*!

Her Royal Highness the Duchess of Cornwall and I first met through our work for the National Osteoporosis Society (NOS), of which I am a patron. Camilla was made President of the Society in October of 2001, in recognition of her tireless work for osteoporosis and her support for the charity. She became a supporter of the charity in 1994, when her mother died as a result of osteoporosis, going on to become a patron three years later. Her first public speech was made in 2002, at the World Congress on Osteoporosis, hosted by the International Osteoporosis Foundation (IOF) in Lisbon. In this speech, she explained why fighting osteoporosis is so important to her.

'My family knew nothing about osteoporosis. The local GP was kind and sympathetic but he, like us, was able to do little to alleviate the terrible pain that my mother suffered so stoically,' she told the audience.

'We watched in horror as she quite literally shrank before our eyes. She lost about eight inches in height and became so bent that she was unable to digest her food properly, leaving her with no appetite at all. In her latter years, she could not breathe without oxygen or even totter round her beloved garden on her Zimmer frame.

'I believe the quality of her life became so dismal and her suffering so unbearable that she just gave up the fight and lost the will to live. As a result of my mother's death, I became determined to find some way of helping people with osteoporosis from experiencing the same fate and general disregard that she encountered.

'I was lucky enough to discover, on my doorstep, the National Osteoporosis Society, a relatively new and small charity, piloted by the indomitable Linda Edwards.'

Her poignant words did much to generate a significant amount of press interest in osteoporosis that year and those in attendance at this event used the occasion to urge policy makers across the globe to make the disease a priority for national health-care agendas.

I have been working with the charity since the summer of 2008, when I co-created the NOS bone-healthy dance, 'Boogie for Your Bones'. And I had the pleasure of being Mr September in the NOS Really Naked Calendar! I led the charity on the Bone Factor Tour, when I visited schools to improve understanding of the need for building strong bones from a young age.

I wanted to do something with my new-found celebrity that would be good for the community but, for me, it had to be a charity where I could make a difference and I knew it had to be about bones as my poor mum has suffered with rheumatoid arthritis for most of her adult life. I have lived through her suffering and pain.

I took one look at the statistics and was compelled to be part of it. One in two women and one in five men over the age of fifty in the UK will fracture a bone, mainly due to poor bone health. People are often unaware that they have fragile bones until the time of a first fracture. Broken wrists, hips and spinal bones are the most common fractures in people with osteoporosis and it is more widespread in older age although younger people can sometimes be affected.

The cause of the disease is still not fully understood, but research continues to build up a picture of the factors that influence our bone health.

During the last few years, we have managed to raise

major sums of money for education and research and have raised the profile of osteoporosis dramatically. On one occasion, I danced with Camilla at a London school where I was teaching the kids how to dance to improve their bone health. Camilla and I danced an impromptu cha-cha-cha together, which was a monumental moment and ended up on the front page of every newspaper the next day, and on the six o'clock news all over the world! My family even saw it in Ballarat, my hometown in Australia, and couldn't believe it. Me dancing with the wife of the future King of England!

Since then, we have become good friends and both work tirelessly for the charity. Our last engagement was a fun one. She came to Oxford to attend a charity night, hosted by me, at my new show *Strictly Confidential*, which had just opened. Camilla had just been riding in the same carriage as the Queen at Ascot and four hours later she was sitting next to me, the other queen.

The proceeds of that evening went to the NOS and raised a staggering £30,000. Camilla is such a delight and always shows great interest when she meets people. She met the show's stars – Lisa Riley, Artem Chigvintsev, Natalie Lowe and Ian Waite – and chatted to the cast after the performance that evening, asking them lots of different questions. The cast were thrilled and left the show on a real high.

In 2011, shortly after her subtle request for tickets in the congratulations letter, Camilla came to the *Strictly* studio to have a look around backstage, see a dress run of the show and meet all the cast, crew, lighting and sound operators, cameramen and woman, TV execs, producers, hosts, judges – in fact, everyone who makes *Strictly* happen live on a Saturday night. We even sat at the judge's desk and held up scores to one of the couples dancing.

Before the scoring, she leaned across to me and said, 'Is it worth a ten?'

'No, darling,' I replied. 'There were a few mistakes. I'd go for a nine.' It was only for fun and she got right into the spirit of it. So our 9 paddles were presented and everyone was delighted. Anita Dobson's famous grin was wider than ever as Camilla stepped over to have a word with her.

It's fantastic that *Strictly* has given me the opportunity to do this sort of work and not only raise the profile of the NOS but other charities I support, which include Macmillan Cancer Support, due to some of my best friends and relatives sadly losing their battle with the disease. What's horrific is one in three of us will get cancer and it's the toughest thing most of us will ever face. If you've been diagnosed with cancer, or a loved one has, you'll want a team of people in your corner supporting you every step of the way. Macmillan provides practical, medical and financial support and push for better cancer care.

Teach First is another charity I support, and their vision is that no child's educational success is limited by their socio-economic background. They train and support people with leadership potential to become inspirational teachers in schools in low income communities across the UK. These teachers change lives. They help young people believe in themselves, and empower them to build a future they may not have believed possible. Each year, a new group of trainees join Teach First and thier university partners for six weeks of intensive training before teaching in one of their partner schools for at least two years, where they achieve a Post Graduate Certificate in Education (PGCE).

I love working with Teach First, it's a charity that works so hard to give opportunities to young people.

Their training and passion for educational equality means that they are dedicated to raising the aspirations of the young people in their classrooms. More than half of those who successfully complete the two-year programme continue to teach. Others go on to work in different sectors of society with similar aims. Some set up social enterprises, some become school governors and others champion the importance of education within policy or business. All are committed to supporting young people achieve, not just in the classroom, but in life.

I have visited many schools all over the country and used my theatre training to inspire and develop leadership qualities within them.

The *Strictly* class of 2011 were an eclectic bunch and there were some very strong personalities, including Edwina Currie and Nancy Dell'Olio.

Edwina was hilarious because, in every single dance, she was trying to be sexy. I think she thought the same thing would happen for her that did with Ann, and she'd get the comedy vote, even though she's a much better dancer than Ann. In the end, she tried a little bit too hard. She was like a cougar on heat around poor Vincent Simone, the young Italian hunk, and it was all a bit grim to watch. But she was always very enthusiastic, and that's what I love in a contestant. I can't promote that enough.

There was a lot of sparkle and enthusiasm that year – not least from Anita Dobson and Russell Grant, who were brimming with it. The show changed Russell's life. He lost loads of weight and got some good jobs out of it and he hasn't stopped working. Flavia did a wonderful job with him, getting him fired out of a cannon, sitting on the bucking Bronco and all that. He became a proper comedy act. That can get a bit tiresome by week eight but he was an infectiously bubbly guy and he loved every minute.

Anita was fabulous, and it was lovely having someone with that amount of grace and class and style on the show. Like Russell, she couldn't get enough of the dancing and threw herself into it with every fibre of her being.

TV presenter Dan Lobb was the other extreme, sadly. I felt that he treated it like it was all below him and I didn't feel that he ever really wanted to be there. He didn't like the criticism and when he got kicked out in week three, he started slagging the show off. When I heard he was on it, I had thought he was really cute and I couldn't wait to see him on the show, but he turned into a bit of a monster.

It was wonderful to meet Lulu on the show but there was a bit of tension between her and Brendan at the beginning, because she made no secret of that fact that she was disappointed that she got him as a dance partner. Her face was a picture at the launch show and she said, 'Oh, no!'

I think he took offence to that, secretly, and that made his life a little bit more difficult.

Alex Jones was very sweet but she got really upset because I said she was 'sexless' in her rumba. James Jordan was piling it on, saying I'm not allowed to say that sort of thing, but actually the dance felt exactly that – cold and sexless. You have to act through dance, and exude certain emotions and sexuality is one of them, particularly in the dance of love. She had some really nice dances as well, and she was adorable. I've been on *The One Show* since and she and Matt couldn't be nicer.

Holly Valance I absolutely loved and she had a great pairing with Artem. I expected her to be really supermodelish and unfriendly, but actually she was completely the opposite. She's a real earth mother, and completely grounded – but then she is a fellow Aussie.

Speaking of Australians, Jason Donovan came third in that series, bless him. He's not the best dancer in the world but he strived and strived, and worked tirelessly to the point of distraction so he got to exactly the right point. His fellow finalists, actress Chelsee Healey and Harry Judd from McFly, were better dancers but Jason worked as hard as anyone could and put in some amazing routines.

On the tour that year, our rooms were opposite each other in the hotel in Nottingham and the walls were really thin. I kept hearing all this warbling coming out of a room, someone singing songs at the top of their voice, and I thought, 'Who the hell is in there?' It was Jason practising for his new album, all day every day, in between the live shows. It's not always easy when you have to do that in hotel rooms. I had plans to go back to playing the trumpet, so I took the trumpet on tour with me, but there aren't many times in a day when you can play a loud instrument in a hotel room without annoying the neighbours. But Jason's warbles were reverberating through the whole of the top floor for hours on end, driving me to distraction. In the end, I had to go out and shop, darling, just to get away from it. Hope it sold.

Chelsee was gorgeous, and so sweet with Pasha Kovalev. She was a bundle of joy and never offensive in any way. And Harry, our series nine winner, I love. I think he's absolutely brilliant. His routines had become so polished, by the time he did the tour he danced like a professional, and his quickstep was undeniably the best male quickstep we've ever had. He had swing, he had sway, he had beautiful shaping and that's something that male celebs never, ever, get, so he was absolutely incredible.

He was also very likeable, down-to-earth and grounded, which you wouldn't expect from a drummer in a big band. I took my niece to see McFly in concert and he got her a backstage pass and took her on a tour, which was lovely of him. He doesn't have to say hello and see anyone at his gigs and I know how busy celebs can get, and it's just so refreshing when you meet people like that.

Robbie Savage turned out to be a great laugh, although I didn't get on with him at the beginning. He was very upset after the first show because of what I'd said to him and because of my scoring and he really did take it to heart. You wouldn't think a rough, tough footballer would be so upset, but he's really sensitive. Back in the hotel room, I was told he rang his mum and he was crying about how I was treating him, but they got to week ten and that was fantastic.

The following January, I took him on tour because he was a real bright spark and so full of personality. He and Ola were a good combination and we became good mates in the end. During the series, the judges can't befriend anyone, because it might influence your judgement, so it was good to get to know him on tour and have a few beers with him.

In Cardiff, I took him and Nancy Dell'Olio to a gay club called the Wow Bar. Wild night. They'd roped off a whole VIP section for us and we were dancing and drinking champagne, then I got up to sing with the drag queens. All these gorgeous young men were coming over to have photos with us and I was snogging randoms all over the place. I was terrible that night!

There was one really gorgeous guy who was pretty keen and we were clearly both attracted to each other and I did a *very* bad thing – I lied about my age. He was twenty-six, so I told him I was thirty! Mind you, he knew who I was, so he only had to look online to find out I was in my late forties. It's all on Wikipedia.

He probably knew I was lying but they don't care at the time, they just know who I am and want to get to know me. But he was lovely, very, very sweet and it was all a bit embarrassing because I was in a gay club with champagne-swigging fag hag Nancy Dell'Olio and ultra-straight Robbie Savage – who was hanging all kinds of crap on me for letting the guy into the VIP area!

Anyway, I thought he was cute and, because he was giving me the eye, I chatted to him and we started kissing. But I saw sense before it went to far and decided it would be wise to get out of there quick. And very unwise to sleep with someone that I didn't know. I'm just not into that, I'm more of a relationship man, but a few Moëts had been sunk at the time.

Robbie was loving it. The clubbers were all over him like a rash, we had to get a security guard to stop people coming through the VIP thing, but it was a really, really funny night. I'm sure that it was Robbie's first experience of a gay club – and probably his last! But Nancy was right at home, swigging her champagne and lapping up the attention.

Nancy made me laugh so much. She was just too much for television really – like Britain's answer to Sophia Loren but more over the top. She was hilarious on the tour and we played up to her diva image. It was the first time I'd used two boys to dance with anyone – she had Robin and Artem carrying her on stage, on a throne, before doing the number with her. It was very funny.

We developed a sort of 'going out' relationship together once the series was over. She would ring me and say, 'Do you want to come to this opening night? Do you want to come to that opening night?' I accompanied her to a few bashes, but I was always left on the wayside while she had all her pictures taken on the red carpet and they weren't particularly interested in me. She's much more interesting because she's like a modern-day courtesan. But I do love her because she's really generous, she's flamboyant, she lives in her own fabulous world and she's completely and utterly full of herself – which I also love. She has an entourage of queens hanging around her and the most outrageous dress sense, and she's hilariously funny, so we get on really well.

On tour, she always has champagne in her dressing room before the show, during the show and after the show, and was always inviting the select few up to her suite. She travels like a Hollywood star, with ten bags of luggage – all matching of course – and at the hotels, she wasn't happy unless she had the penthouse or the big fabulous corner suite. The company provides the basic room but she upgraded herself in every single place.

Nancy – lovely, generous, flamboyant – fab-u-lous!

In July 2012, we were both invited to *Strictly* dancer Katya Virshilas's wedding, to Danish dancer Klaus Kongsdal, in the south of France. *Hello!* magazine was doing a spread on it but Nancy only appears in one shot because, in typical diva style, she arrived three days late!

I was already going to be in Paris, so I arranged to meet Nancy there and have dinner with her on the Thursday night, before travelling down, the following day, to the hotel where the wedding was taking place. It was all arranged, Nancy was getting the Eurostar, and she'd booked all our accommodation.

'OK, darling,' I said, 'dinner in Paris, then on Friday we'll get down to the hotel and have a gorgeous spa day there and lord it up, do the pre-wedding champagne evening with the bride and groom and be relaxed and ready for the actual wedding day, on Saturday.' We had decided that one the Sunday we would both chill at the hotel, have a lovely time and then travel back to Paris on the Sunday evening ready to come back to London on Monday.

So on Thursday, Nancy rang.

'Craig, dah-ling,' she breathed down the phone, in her dramatic drawl. 'I cannot meet you for dinner. I cannot get to Paris until Friday. I'll see you then.'

'Oh, OK, fine,' I said. Then I began to wonder how I would get to the wedding venue, as we were supposed to be travelling down together in a car, and because she was single and I was single, we were each other's plus ones. But she said, 'I may have met someone, I cannot meet you tonight for dinner in Paree.'

'That's all right, darling,' I told her. 'I'll amuse myself, I have loads of friends here.' So I went out with some people I know in Paris and all was well.

The following morning, Nancy called again.

'Craig, dah-ling, I cannot come. I have an important meeting now today, so I will be see you on Saturday,' she said.

'Well, hang on, no,' I said. 'But Nancy, we're meant to be travelling down together.'

'Oh, I know, dah-ling, I know!'

'I thought we were going down by car from Paris,' I said.

'Oh no, no, no. I come now later.' But she wasn't sure what she was doing so it was all up in the air.

'Darling,' I said. 'I'll get on the train and get a taxi from there and I'll meet you at the hotel. So you do what you have to do, get on the Eurostar to Paris, and then you can get one down to the Loire Valley and I'll meet you there.

'I'm leaving the hotel at seven o'clock, if you're there, at the hotel that you've booked for me, we will leave together and go to the champagne reception, then you'll be all fine for the wedding, you can get made up and your hair done and the frock done, all on Saturday morning at the hotel.'

She didn't make it Friday night either! I went to the champagne reception on my own.

'Where's Nancy?' asked Katya.

I replied, 'She hasn't shown up.'

We had a fabulous time at the pre-wedding drinks do and then I went back to the hotel. No Nancy. No message. Nothing.

The following morning, I got a call.

'Dah-ling, I'm going to be on the nine o'clock train to Paris, and then from Paris I get the car and I will be with you before you leave for the wedding.'

The magazine photoshoot started at two in the afternoon and Katya wanted us there for that. So Nancy was due to arrive in Paris at 11 a.m., an hour down, arrive at twelve, do her hair, make-up, frock and get to the venue by two for the *Hello!* photoshoot and the all-important actual wedding, which was at four o'clock.

It was a beautiful day. The wedding was in the most beautiful setting, the Château de Chissay in the Loire Valley. Katya looked stunning and it was all gorgeous. But no Nancy. Then we found out her hairdresser and make-up artist – who she was bringing over from London – was waiting at Eurostar for her at nine o'clock to get on the train, with all her bags of rollers, make-up etc. – and Nancy missed the sodding train.

The hairdresser waited and waited, and she eventually turned up at midday. I got another call, at lunchtime, saying, 'Ah dah-ling, don't worry. I will be there.'

So what time did she finally arrive? She arrived as the speeches were starting, at 7.30 that night! She whirled in with a loud, 'Dah-ling!' and expecting a huge fanfare. It was the funniest thing. We'd been there two days, we'd been to the wedding, we'd done the photoshoots and she drops in at 7.30 p.m., leaves at 11 and that was the last I saw of her that night. She didn't stay to dance or anything.

We were both put on the same table together with Holly Valance, but I had a spare chair next to me all afternoon. Because Katya's husband is Danish, the whole family speaks and there's a play reading, so the speeches went on from seven to midnight. Nancy was huffing and puffing through the whole thing. 'Oh, not another tiring speech! Oh, will they ever stop speaking?'

The food didn't come out and the speeches were well underway and so the main course was served at nine o'clock. The best man was trying to deliver his speech while the waiters were serving, which was a bit chaotic but, by this time, Holly and I were absolutely slaughtered because we'd been drinking since two, and we hadn't eaten anything all day.

Anyway, we had planned to spend Sunday there, but I decided to go back to Paris instead.

'Darling, what are you doing?' I asked Nancy, 'because I'm going back to Paris.'

'Oh, no,' she replied. 'I booked the Sunday here.'

'But there's no one staying at the hotel on Sunday, so you'll just be here by yourself,' I told her, thinking she'd have known that if she'd bothered to turn up any earlier.

'Oh, well, maybe I'll come back then,' she decided. 'But I'm not ready to go.'

'I'm going now because I've booked a train that I'm going to go back on and I've got this taxi arriving,' I said, and I left her to it. But it didn't end there. I got the train back, she was getting a car back later. The driver that had been driving us all around was driving Nancy back – she basically commandeered the wedding chauffeur and convinced him to take her to Paris. I was on the 5.15 from Paris to London and she said she would be on that one too, but I left thinking I wouldn't see Nancy again, at least not this side of the English Channel.

Sure enough, I got to the Gare du Nord and, surprise, surprise, no Nancy. I wasn't going to wait, so I started going through immigration.

I was just about to show my passport and I heard, 'Craig, Craig, Craig. Dah-ling.'

She came screaming from the end of the concourse, rushing towards me in a panic, and she said she'd just arrived and she'd missed the check-in for that train, so they wouldn't let her on. I was in the queue at immigration, and she was trapped on the other side of the glass partition. They had my passport and when they gave it back to me I had to move on, so all I could do was wave at her and say, 'See you in London, darling.' Her face was a picture!

She is a total character. She's loveable, funny, but just completely scatty. And after that experience, I won't be making travel plans with her ever again. Now I know what Anton was going through during the show, I feel quite sorry for him. It's a wonder she ever showed up for training!

# CHAPTER 7

# THERE IS NOTHING LIKE A DAME

After our *Strictly* tour triumph, I decided to ask Ann Widdecombe to join me in panto. I was still playing the Wicked Queen and there was a part as my hapless servant, which could easily be adapted to suit her. So, after the show one night, as the tour was drawing to a close, I approached her in the bar over a Sauvignon Blanc and asked her if she would consider it. To my surprise she leapt at the idea, and was so enthusiastic I had to try and calm her down, because I hadn't mentioned it to the production team behind the panto. The following morning she was ringing me to ask whether I'd talked to them yet – she was so keen.

Luckily, the producer thought it was a cracking idea and at Christmas 2011, at the Orchard Theatre in Dartford, Ann became my 'Widdy in Waiting'.

Panto is an art form and not any old celeb can pull it off, but there's an added art in playing yourself, which is not as easy as you may think. Ann had a lot of lines to learn and it's difficult for a non-actor to take direction, but she threw herself into the part and she did it surprisingly well. After years as a famous MP, she also added political clout, which made the topical jokes in the script much funnier. By the end of the run, she was so confident, she was giving me her own notes on the dances!

By now, I knew exactly what to expect from my panto run and I had started to really enjoy it. At some point in the previous season it had clicked and I realized I could be a lot more free with it. I had approached my first panto like a great Shakespearian role. I wanted to be a good actor and I wanted to be professional, but I took it too seriously and that was my downfall. People love it when you come out of character and actually it helps, because otherwise people don't recognize who you are. So I started putting some of my own jokes in, and adding a few topical lines, and I just became more and more confident with it.

The voice of the magic mirror had been provided, for the first two years, by Paul O'Grady, then, when we moved to Dartford, by *Strictly*'s very own Len Goodman. During one show, I said, 'Mirror, mirror on the wall, who's the fairest of them all?' and there was no Len Goodman. Nothing. So I had to act to a blank mirror and try to tell the audience what was going on, and I was trying to remember his lines as well as my lines. It was a nightmare.

'Darlings,' I said. 'I think we have a slight technical hitch with my little magic mirror. She's not being very magic!' It was very funny, but you have to get around those situations.

Len came see the panto in Dartford, his hometown, and he sat in the audience watching himself as the mirror. I told the audience he was watching and they gave him a round of applause, which he loved. He came backstage and said, 'I should be paid more for that!'

Ann and I got used to working with one another and we had a real laugh. She was an enormous amount of fun, which is a side of her that not many people see. We're billed as arch enemies, and that's the act, but, in fact, nothing could be further from the truth.

In one number, I had to lift her up and spin her, before throwing her to the ground, violently enough to make her slide four or five feet across the floor. She was covered in bruises but she soldiered on for most of the run. But after thirty-two of the forty-two performances, we were forced to change the routine – my back and Ann's bruises could take no more.

We came up with a new lift, where I would hook my arms underneath her armpits and spin her around, although I still had to throw her onto the floor, for comic effect. It all went well in rehearsal, before we were in costume, but I hadn't bargained for my triple G-cup fake boobs. By the time I had the boobs and high heels on, I was about a foot away from her, and I couldn't get in the right position.

During one performance, I actually exclaimed, 'Aaargh!' during the lift and, afterwards, she said, 'Are you all right?'

'It's OK,' I lied. 'I was just acting.' But my poor back could have done with one of the Wicked Queen's magic potions by the time that run was over.

On 2 January, barely a week after Harry Judd had lifted the *Strictly* glitterball trophy, I opened the papers to find that Alesha Dixon had quit the show. I was utterly dumbfounded. She must have been plotting the move all the way through and, even after the series wrapped and we all said our goodbyes, she didn't breathe a word.

Alesha has every right to move on; I wish her all the luck in the world. I was just upset that she didn't call or text me, even after it became public, to say, 'It's been great working with you guys, but I'm leaving to join the Cowell camp.'

Dear Alesha had a hard time when she started on *Strictly*, but soon got into her stride.

I was really upset because for three years I'd been tirelessly defending her, which wasn't always easy, especially for the first year, when every single interview was about Arlene and Alesha. Then, after three years, it would have been nice to get a text message to say, 'I'm going to *Britain's Got Talent*,' or, 'It's been nice working with you. Thank you.' Anything like that would be good. But nothing – absolutely nothing! Even when *Britain's Got Talent* was on, and I saw her being introduced as the new judge, I was thinking, 'Still not heard a word from her'.

There are many reasons why Simon Cowell might want to employ Alesha, but I'm pretty sure it's mainly because she was on *Strictly*. There's this on-going feud between the commercial stations and the BBC, particularly between *The X Factor* and *Strictly Come Dancing*, who are vying for the Saturday-night figures. Before *Strictly*, Alesha's career was in the doldrums (I mean, who remembers the hits of Mystique?) and she was trying to make a comeback as a solo artist. She was always ambitious and I think she used the show to raise her profile and now she's doing what she's better at, which is talking about pop acts and novelties.

Despite the rivalries, Simon Cowell is quite good friends with Bruno and they text chat all the time. When they are filming in the US, Bruno and Len's trailer is next to Simon Cowell's because they film the *American Idol* and *Dancing With the Stars* at the same studios and so he stands out there smoking fags with Bruno. I have met him through Bruno and he was nice, absolutely fine. I don't have any rivalry with him at all, so none of that's an issue. We are all doing the same thing really, judging competitions, but mine's dance and his is song. The fact he makes billions out of it, well, lucky him!

One of the weirder jobs I landed in 2012 was a BBC1 show called *The Magicians*, which saw me plummeting off a cliff while locked in the boot of a car – filmed as live TV in one take.

The show has magicians and celebrities performing tricks and I was pitted against David Hasselhoff and the *Countryfile* presenter Julia Bradbury. I had to pull off a pirate dance card trick, got my head chopped off and performed a trick inside a giant balloon in a shopping centre in Bristol.

This massive balloon was blown up and I had to climb inside it, then it was tied off and I was locked in and running out of air. They took a shopper's credit card, which was somehow passed through the latex and, when they popped the balloon, it was in my hand. It was an amazing trick. But it took some preparation and just getting into the balloon was a nightmare, because my shoulders are so broad and I was trying to wiggle in. I had to have a rehearsal added to that, I was a nervous wreck because I'm a bit claustrophobic.

Having my head chopped off could have gone horribly wrong, because it's a real blade, which is amazing. But there was a much more terrifying stunt to come. The two magicians I was working with, Barry Jones and Stuart MacLeod, told me I was going to do the 'Exploding Car Trick'.

They took me to a huge quarry in the south west of

England and told me, 'We're going to tie you up and bundle you into the boot of the car. The car is going to start rolling towards the cliff edge, where it will topple off, and fall 100 feet into the water below. You need to escape from the car and leap onto a queen-sized mattress and once you've escaped, the car, which we've needlessly laced with explosives, will race down and career off the cliff edge.'

A group of my 'fans' had gathered to watch the stunt live, to ensure there was no camera trickery. So they handcuffed my wrists, put gaffer tape over my mouth and around my ankles and a bag over my head, then shoved me into the boot. A brick was put on the accelerator of the car, so it would travel at fifteen mph, and they explained that I had ten seconds to escape, adding, 'If Craig doesn't manage to escape, we have arranged a party in his honour. Ann Widdecombe has already sent out the invites.' The things you do for money!

We had four false starts and the safety mechanisms kept going wrong, so it was making me really nervous. The trick had to be done in daylight and by this time the sun was going down, so we were running literally to the last second. To prove there was no clever editing, the whole stunt had to be filmed in one take, and this was the last possible take. I was absolutely terrified that I might actually go to my death … on TV.

Of course, we passed the mattress, with me still in the boot and the two guys getting increasingly frantic, and then the car went over the cliff and exploded. For a few seconds, the poor people on the bank must have thought they'd seen me die, because you couldn't see me get out of the car. Then I appeared in the door of the helicopter above the explosion – alive and well.

Sadly, I can't tell you how it was done – except that it involved a lot of running – but it was one of the most expensive tricks that they've ever achieved on the show and it was an incredibly exhilarating experience for me.

A week after I split from Grant, in the autumn of 2011, I had really needed someone to talk to so I called Doctor D to pour my heart out. We had briefly dated in the wake of my break-up with Lloyd, seven years earlier, but it hadn't worked out and we had since become friends. We didn't see each other often because he lived out of London but he sometimes came to watch *Strictly*, and he had met Grant on several occasions. I told him about the split and he said, 'Maybe I'll come down and visit you in London.' A month later, he did just that and we had a really great time, so we started seeing each other again. I was delighted, because he was gorgeous, but I didn't think of it as being anything long-term. This time, the second time around, I was going to try and build on the relationship and get to know him a little bit more.

We saw each other several times and then he suggested maybe we should go for a weekend away, so I said, 'Yes, that sounds great. Let's book something.'

As my stint on *Strictly* goes straight into the tour after Christmas, I like to book a holiday in February so I can squeeze in some relaxation between the tour and my theatre work, which often takes up the spring and summer. I was travelling around the country, on the 2012 tour, and we were talking all the time on the telephone, so I broached the subject of a holiday.

'Let's go somewhere really nice and hot and sunny,' I said. 'How about the Maldives, or St Lucia, for two weeks?'

'I can't get that much time off work,' he said; so I opted for a seven-day break and he said, 'That might be all right.'

I sent him lots of flight details and lots of ideas about where we could go, and then he said, 'Actually, I'd really rather make it just a weekend.'

'But I've got two weeks off that I need to fill and I was rather hoping we could spend it together, seeing we're sort of – together.'

Then I thought, 'Are we together, or are we not?' It was never really said. It was one of those sort of odd moments where something has been planted in my mind and I haven't actually asked whether it's true or not.

A couple of days later, I called him from Nottingham and said, 'Look, I've got this flight, can you get the seven days off?'

'I'll call you back within the hour,' he said. Then he called back and said, 'I can't come.'

'OK,' I said, as my heart sank to my stomach. It had happened again. He'd gone cold on me, just like the last time. I was devastated. For the next few days, I stayed in my hotel room, only emerging for the show. I couldn't believe how upset I was and I didn't hear anything from him for the rest of the tour.

As soon as the tour ended, I went on holiday by myself for the first time ever. I booked a fortnight in St Lucia and I thought, 'Right, Craig, it's time to grow up. It's time for you to take control of your own life and not rely on anyone else to be there for you.'

I began to realize that I was on the rebound from Grant, and I was pretending that I was sane and centred, but actually I needed to do the same thing that Grant was doing – I needed to learn to be on my own. There was me preaching to Grant, like the font of all knowledge, but of course I needed to become self-sufficient as well. The first time I had met Doctor D, seven years earlier, I had been on date frenzy because I was desperate to find someone to fill the gap left by Lloyd and, this time, I had been trying to fill the Grant space. Isn't that just horrible? But, at the same time, I knew there was something special about Doctor D and I was really upset that it had failed again. I even booked two seats on the flight to St Lucia, in the vain hope he would change his mind.

I was really nervous about going away on my own but I bravely faced the BA flight, by myself, to an all-inclusive, activity-based holiday destination that sounded like everything I hate. All the way there I was thinking, 'This is going to be just ghastly.'

I had booked the Penthouse Suite, which was Caribbean luxury at its finest. It had a private entry staircase on the fourth floor, leading to the only suite on the fifth floor. It had an open floor plan with a large living area and wet bar and the bathroom boasted a soaking tub for two, which is elevated on a tiled platform, so you can sit in the tub and enjoy spectacular views over the ocean.

The suite's *pièce de résistance* was the private Hammam, or Turkish bath, which featured a marble-slab heated massage bed and marble benches, plus a steam room. It was stunning.

As soon as I arrived, I thought, 'This would have been so nice if we'd been together.' But I gave myself a stern talking too and settled in.

'Right,' I told myself, 'I'm going to get myself together, exercise and do classes all day.' Because it was a BodyHoliday – run by LeSport – there was plenty to do. And while I had dreaded every minute, it turned out to be just what I needed. I came away having lost a stone in weight and looking and feeling so much better, which was just brilliant.

One thing I hadn't bargained for was that everybody in the resort was British, so everyone knew who I was. I never thought anyone in St Lucia would know me, but when I arrived there, everyone was going, 'Oh, my God, it's Craig Revel Horwood from *Strictly Come Dancing*!' Of course, they were all the right demographic of the show's core audience, so it was like a *Strictly* fanfest. At first, I thought this was the worst-case scenario, like being stuck with five hundred fans – on the beach, in the bar, at breakfast, at lunch, at dinner – but actually it was sensational.

Everyone was so nice to me, and the celebrity thing turned out to be a bonus because I could just go up to tables and say, 'Hi, how you doing?' and people were interested and keen to talk, so I was kept occupied the entire time.

In the end, we had a real laugh and I loved it. It was brilliant speaking to the fans and, after lots of photos, initially, it calmed down and people just said, 'Hi Craig'. I got to know a lot of the singles there and one in particular, a lady doctor called Nikki, has become a very good friend of mine. We had some mad nights in the spa bath there. It was all a bit racy, the whole thing – three o'clock in the morning drinking champagne round the spa, footballers' wives and all sorts of shenanigans. And I loved it!

Being single on holiday certainly has its advantages. It's obvious really, you're not with anybody so you can make up your own mind how long you stay somewhere and what you want to do the next day. I learned to be by myself. I learned to read books again. I'm always reading scripts and anything that's attached to shows that I'm doing, but not novels. And it was really wonderful to go on holiday and meet other singles – because I hadn't considered myself single up to that point. Isn't that funny?

Following my citizenship study and my driving test, I continued my learning frenzy by earning a scuba-diving open-water certificate, from the Professional Association of Diving Instructors (PADI). I didn't realize when I signed up for it, how much study was involved. I just got up one morning and thought, 'Maybe I ought to try a bit of scuba-diving, as I've never done it.' When I spoke to the instructor he said, 'Do you want go scuba diving for one day or do you want to do open water, which allows you to go out with loads of other people and scuba dive all over the world?' I thought it seem a great shame not to do the whole thing, so I just paid for the whole session. I had no clue what it entailed, though.

You have to do five dives and then a three-hour written test so there was a *lot* of studying. And you can't drink, so it's no wonder I lost weight! I didn't realize that booze was banned until I read the book and I thought, 'Oh, no, this has ruined my holiday!' But actually it *made* it because it gave me something to aim for and something to achieve.

I was quite nervous about going underwater, because I'm a little bit claustrophobic, and it was scary to start with, especially when I had to practice all the emergency procedures. The most urgent emergencies in scuba diving generally involve loss of breathing, gas-supply failures, situations where breathing air is likely to run out before the diver can surface, or inability to ascend, and uncontrolled ascents. This particular test was for a controlled emergency swimming ascent. For that, I was completely submerged ten feet under and I had to take off my half mask and pull the regulator – the small piece of apparatus that connects to the back-mounted gas cylinder and the mouthpiece – out of my mouth. Then I had to try to find it all and put it all back on blind, clearing the mask of water, before shooting up to the surface in an emergency ascent. I had to do that five times before they'd pass me, because I was so nervous I kept getting it wrong. The second time I attempted the manoeuvre, I accidentally breathed in through my nose breathing water into my lungs and began to cough, I had no mask on, ten feet below the surface, no regulator in which to breath – you could say I went into a mild hysteria for a split second but because you're so well trained your training and the need to survive kicked in. I found my regulator and slowed down and regulated my breathing coughing out the salt water that had entered my lungs while pinching my nose. Once that was under control, I searched for my mask – all the time blind – then proceeded to place the mask on, clearing the mask of water by pushing out air from my nose then making my way to the surface. Eeeek!

At that point, I truly did not want to do it again but my instructor signalled to repeat the exercise which I bravely did, three more times, until I felt confident and comfortable with the routine. But I passed the course and really enjoyed it.

After a great fortnight, when I'd had a ball and met some really good friends, I prepared to travel back to my empty house – but I was no longer scared. I remember walking through the door and thinking, 'I'm all right! I'm not breaking down in tears, I'm not collapsing in a screaming heap by the fire, or drowning my sorrows in red wine.' Just two weeks away had made me totally prepared and ready to come back to live in a house by myself without feeling afraid or alone. It felt really, really good.

As soon as I came back from St Lucia, I started filming *Maestro at the Opera*, which entailed three months of intense study of Puccini, Verdi and Mozart. I was learning to become a conductor and I was absorbed in music and really enjoying myself. Quite late in life, I was becoming addicted to learning and I was doing all the things that I'd been putting off for years – becoming a British citizen, learning to drive, learning a new talent – and I'd even gone beyond with the scuba diving.

*Maestro*, however, did present me with a family problem. Some time before, I had arranged to go to Australia in March and April, to spend some time with mum and all the family. I thought I was free because, although I had had a meeting about the programme in June, the producers told me I'd know if we were on by September and, when I didn't hear, I assumed it wasn't happening. So I booked a holiday to Australia and I told the whole family, 'I'm coming out this time, I'm not going to accept any work, I won't be doing anything. I promise you I will arrive.' This was the third year running that I'd made a promise to come, so they were all planning parties and visits, and my sister Diane wanted to get married, so she thought this would be the perfect time for the wedding. Then, in December, while I was doing panto, I got the phone call saying that *Maestro* was going ahead from March to May. I was committed to it because I'd already said that I would do it, if it were to come up, but I felt awful.

'Oh, my God,' I thought, 'How am I going to tell my family?' I felt so guilty about not seeing everyone for four years and it was tough calling home to tell them what had happened, but they were really good about it and understood it was something I felt I had to do.

After I explained, I said, 'Listen, this is how we're going to get round this. Mum, you're coming over for two months.' I had flown Mum over every eighteen months, so I could see her, but my little sister Mel was really upset with me.

'I never get to see you,' she said. 'You're always a big let-down.'

'OK, Mel,' I said. 'How about you come over for six weeks as well.' She happily agreed to that plan,

With that to look forward to, I immersed myself in the opera, which kept me occupied for three months and helped me get over another broken relationship. Perhaps that's why I was so passionate about Puccini and *La Bohème* – because love was never far from my mind.

The show pitted my conducting skills against those of actress and comedienne Josie Lawrence, Oxford professor of mathematics Marcus du Sautoy and DJ Trevor Nelson.

After a crash course, the four of us were let loose to conduct an operatic aria in full, with no less than the orchestra at the Royal Opera House – whose talented members would then be the ones eliminating the contestants. It was terrifying, but wonderful and I'm happy to say I went on to win it.

That was a real turning point for me because I felt like I'd achieved something and, looking back over those few months, I thought, 'Actually, Craig you have been living alone for a long time, and you're fine. In fact, you're actually enjoying it.'

*Maestro* was great for me, it was just what I needed at that time in my life. It kept me focused and occupied and I was learning a skill that would prove useful in my directorial and choreographic career. I'd never really considered how difficult it was going to be. As a dancer, I thought I would have an advantage as I had natural rhythm, teamed with the fact that I read music, so I thought it would be a doddle. Nothing could be further from the truth.

Dancers are trained to dance on the beat, not ahead or behind the beat. When you conduct, you have to beat the rhythms out slightly ahead of the beat for certain instruments in order to hear the result of your downbeat at the right time. By the time the sound travels to your ears your downbeat is over and your 'time signature arm', in my case the right arm, is moving on to its next beat. It was like rubbing your tummy in a circular motion and patting your head at the same time. I found it a real challenge and that's what spurred me on. I'm not a person who is fond of failure although I do appreciate that one must fail to succeed and fail I did on a daily basis.

Nothing would have been achieved, however, without the amazing talents of my wonderful tutor and mentor and now good friend, Michael Rosewell. He is Music Director of the English Touring Opera, also Artistic Director of the London Phoenix Ensemble and Director of Opera for the Benjamin Britten International Opera School at the Royal College of Music, London. He is an extremely well-respected and gifted conductor and must have thought he'd been cursed when he landed me as a student. We worked tirelessly together but also had a good time and a laugh along the way. He was a task master but in a gentle and passionate way. We had great respect for one another, which made us a very good team. Also included in that team was our répétiteur, who had to try to replicate with only two hands the sound and feel of an eighty-piece orchestra, playing some of the most difficult passages in classical music for me to conduct. She was also briefed to follow my every move, which she did religiously and to my detriment.

I managed to get through all my heats, albeit crudely at times, and was given the chance to go to Italy to study

Puccini for the final. Marcus and I were the finalists and he was going to be a difficult contestant to beat as he had played in orchestras before, understood that world and was also a very good reader of music. He was also extremely knowledgeable about opera itself and has had a passion for it all his life. We got on very well – but we were in competition and he *really* wanted to win!

Italy was great and we both learned a lot, but it was going into Puccini's house in Lucca that really stood out. As we walked in we both fell still and silent, overawed by the knowledge that we were visiting the very place in which Puccini sat and penned his amazing operas.

Giacomo Puccini was born in Lucca, Italy, on 22 December 1858. He spent his childhood in Lucca and the city embraced him as a favorite native son. His house has been restored in the style of the mid-nineteenth century and made into a small museum that is open to the public. If you're a fan of Puccini and opera, as I am, the house is of huge interest. As a visitor, you're allowed walk through and each room has a small description of what it was used for and the objects in the room (written in both Italian and English, mercifully). On display in the museum are manuscripts and music scores from his operas, photos and paintings, a piano, a costume from an opera, and other memorabilia. The former dining room is now Puccini's grave, with a plaque on the floor.

Marcus and I did lots of filming there for the TV show; we even got to sit on Puccini's piano chair and pretend to play his piano, which was in the front living room. Marcus almost broke the chair by nearly falling off it backwards when he went to sit in it. We both burst into schoolgirl laughter and as it was such a quiet environment, we tried desperately to stifle it … and if that wasn't bad enough, the film crew were filming our reactions to the house, which made it worse.

The *Maestro* experience was opening a world to me that I'd never really known. Yes, I had directed and choreographed operas before but this was real and my knowledge of Puccini's music was becoming greater and greater with every lesson.

I won the final round after a gruelling and nerve-racking session with the amazing Royal Opera House orchestra, who had to vote for who they wanted to conduct them on the night. The votes were cast 65 to 35 in my favour. Now the real work had to begin. I rehearsed relentlessly and, on one particular day at home, I made a breakthrough. I was having trouble with three sections of the act and could not get them right, I'd always go back to the beginning of the piece and if I made a mistake, would stop and start again. This went on for weeks then this day, after a non-stop rehearsal that lasted four hours, I got through the entire piece without a single hiccup. I simply broke down in tears, sobbing uncontrollably, through sheer exhaustion and relief.

After three weeks of intensive rehearsals, I stepped up to the podium to conduct Act II of *La Bohème*, widely considered one of the most difficult acts to conduct in one of the most complex operas ever written. Despite nerves and in front of a two-thousand-strong audience at the Royal Opera House, on Saturday 5 May, I took to the orchestra pit to lead the cast in a seventeen minute act that includes over 200 people on stage, over 1,000 props and a real dog! This had to be my finest twenty minutes, I suppose, ever! There is nothing that can replace the feeling I got from it. The experience was phenomenal in opening the doors to the most wonderful artistic life that you could ever possibly want: opera.

Michael Rosewell, my mentor, said in an interview after the performance, 'Craig was absolutely fantastic. He was in touch with the sentiment and the feelings of the music and his focus was up to the stage, which is something we've been talking about but he's never achieved it. You really felt he was a proper conductor! I'm absolutely delighted.'

I was absolutely thrilled to have had the pleasure of learning under someone so incredible and without him and his enormous patience I never would have got there so, thank you, Michael.

With *Maestro* over, it was time to see the family. Mel came over first and I decided to pick her up from the airport myself. I had only had the driving licence for a few months and I was a bit nervous about driving out to Heathrow, so the day before I had to pick her up I had a practice drive. There are plenty of things you still need to learn after passing your test. For instance, I'd never driven into a car park and paid at the machine, and I'd never used one of those barriers where you insert tickets, so I just wanted to practice how to do all that. You can't go on motorways as a learner either, but I had already taken a motorway driving course, to relieve myself of that worry, so I was fine with that.

The practice run went fine and the next day I drove out again to collect Melanie. It was a really sunny day, it was gorgeous, so I had the roof of the Stag down, which was an absolute delight. Her luggage wouldn't fit in the boot so I put it on the back seat, sticking up, and off we went.

Halfway down the motorway, I drove round a bend and accelerated a little bit fast and, suddenly, we heard crash, bang, bump, thump!

'Aargh,' I shrieked. 'What was that? We thought it was Mel's luggage falling out the back of the car, onto the motorway and but the case was still there. I looked in the road and I just went, 'Oh, my God!' The back end of my car had fallen off!

It was just the metal bumper trimming, but the noise it made was horrible. We were screaming, absolutely screaming. I saw it in the rear view mirror being mangled by other cars running over it, but at least we still had the suitcase. Melanie and I laughed hysterically all the way back home, so it was a hilarious start to her stay.

For the first time in years, I'd taken the summer off from the Watermill Theatre and I wasn't doing any theatrical projects. So when Melanie arrived, we went on a little holiday with my new friend Nikki – who I met in St Lucia. We went to Sicily – on Bruno's recommendation for ten days, and it was glorious. It was great to have Mel, who is beyond a wild girl and Nikki in my company and to go somewhere I'd never been before. I rented a beautiful two-bed apartment overlooking the sea, and it was hot, with a gorgeous beach just a two minute walk through the town. We assumed a position on sun loungers and didn't really move from them for the full ten days. The eye candy was amazing, all those Italian boys with tattoos in their Speedos. We were in heaven.

We all decided to have henna tattoos on the beach, the semi-permanent ones that wash off after a week or so. Nikki had a motif placed on her hip, Mel had a sunburst in the small of her back, I had a tribal-style pattern around my biceps. We loved ourselves sick with them, so decided on the second to last day of the holiday to have them redone so we could show them off with our tans back home. This particular day, we'd had a boozy lunch, then staggered to the beach to have them painted on. I decided to go all out and have a massive Maori tribal design all over my right calf muscle plus a massive spider on my right shoulder and then, finally, my bicep tattoo redone. Nikki had hers redone and Mel decided to go all out and add a full sleeve one on her arm. They take a while to do and you have to lay still and let them dry for an hour. After the hour, you peel the gluey residue off and it reveals a very realistic-looking tattoo.

Well … Mel was so drunk she couldn't sit still and smudged her full sleeve before it had time to dry. She then lost her balance, necking another cocktail, and fell backwards off the sun-lounger, both legs in the air in her bikini I might add, smearing the 'henna' all over her body. Nikki and I were killing ourselves laughing, as they stain instantly for at least a week. You can't wash them off as they fade in time. When Mel recovered drunkenly from her legs akimbo moment, we noticed the black ink was smudged all over her face as well, where she'd tried to break her fall. She was one big mess of smudged black henna and it was going to be there for the following week. To cap it all, we had a red-carpet event to attend on our return the following evening. We laughed and laughed until our stomachs cramped, all the way back to London.

Three days later, I got my comeuppance when I had an extremely bad reaction. The ink they use is often just cheap black hair dye rather than the natural reddish-brown colouring that has been used for cultural festivals in areas of Africa and Asia for centuries. I later discovered that the coal-tar hair dye contains p-phenylenediamine (PPD), an ingredient that can cause dangerous skin reactions in some people and is banned from use in cosmetics that are intended to be applied to the skin. I had an allergy to the mix. My new gorgeous tattoos began to blister and itch ... I was covered in raised red weeping lesions.

I had been absolutely fine after the first one at the beginning of the holiday but apparently if too much PPD is used some peoples skin flares up. Nikki and Mel had no reaction at all with their tattoos and managed to get the last laugh on me. I went to my local GP and was refered to a skin specialist, terrified I would be left with permanent scarring and have no other option to cover them with real tattoos. I applied some creams to them, to no avail.

It did stop the itching but in the end it actually did leave some nasty scarring! Thankfully, the scars have now faded somewhat – unlike the memory.

When we got back to London, my mum came over, so we had a crossover period, with my mother and sister both staying with me. While she was here, Mel met up with a boyfriend whom she knew from Australia, but who had moved to the UK. He soon decided to move back to Australia, and they are now living together.

Mum was over for two months, so I took her on little trips because, for the first time, I had the car and could drive her around the country. It was a really lovely break and I loved having her around.

I hear there is a world shortage of fake tan – can't imagine why … *Above:* Vincent Simone and *left:* Artem Chigvintsev – one of my stars in *Strictly Confidential.*

*acing page*: On 19 June 2013 we staged the Gala performance of Strictly
Confidential. Camilla, Duchess of Cornwall did me the great honour of attending,
and we raised £30,000 for the National Osteoporosis Society (AFP/Getty Images).

*bove*: The cast of the show and I meet Camilla after a sold out performance
Getty Images).

*Above*: He's behind you!!! I'm used to being booed on live television but doing panto takes it to a whole new level!

*Below*: Chilli Cha Cha Cha Sausage anyone?!

ne fantastic Ann Widdecombe as Widdy in Waiting and me as the Wicked Queen
just as well we never got our costumes mixed up! (Getty Images)

Zöe Lucker

Russell Grant

Kelly Brook

Matt Baker
and Mum

Lulu and Ann
Widdecombe

Nicky Byrne

As I said, *Strictly* is the best Saturday job a man – or woman – could have! (© BBC)

# CHAPTER 8

# DARCEY BUSSELLS IN

I n April 2012, it was announced that Darcey Bussell was to join us on the *Strictly* panel and the three of us couldn't have been more delighted. She had already been a guest judge, for a few weeks in 2009, and had been a big hit. Plus, she had excellent dance credentials and, being the UK's most famous Prima Ballerina, she would add touch of class to proceedings.

Before Darcey did the show for real, we had a mini run-through, to teach her the ropes a little bit, and make her feel a little bit more confident and comfortable. They set up a judging desk in one of the offices of the BBC, and they gave us videos to watch, and we commented to see how the banter might go and how she would react in a live situation. Although she had guested, it's still a bit daunting sitting on the desk for the first time as a permanent judge so they wanted to see how she was going to be and to give her a little more of an insight into how to judge and what points she should be looking for.

One of the hardest things to get right is keeping your comments to ten seconds, or whatever time constraint you are given. As I am about to speak, I'm told, 'Craig, you've got ten seconds on this one' or 'You've got thirty seconds.' You have to know how long a minute is, or how long thirty seconds of speaking time is, because you can get carried away and neglect to get the timings right. There are two minutes for all four judges to speak, so generally it should be thirty seconds each, but if Brucie's jokes go on a bit long, or if they go down well and he adds to them, or Bruno rambles on a bit, it's up to the rest of us to truncate the time, and be as brief and concise as we can.

On top of that, we need to make sure we are not all of the same opinion, because it would be terrible if we all said exactly the same thing about the dancing. Luckily, Darcey comes from a very different form of dance, classical ballet, and so we're all from different walks of life in the dance world, which makes it work.

The first session was a bit ropey. I did that with her

because I knew Darcey a little bit. I've choreographed *The Ballet Boys*, and I've done ballets for opera, so our paths had crossed. She didn't need a lot of coaching but I was there just to help her along and make a few suggestions. I told her, 'You have to be strong of opinion, that's the important thing.' We just gave her enough confidence to go on into the live show. It is difficult when a camera is put in your face and you know that there are fourteen million viewers. Whatever comes out of your mouth is going to be there for ever, and probably printed in the paper the next day, and because live and it's not pre-scripted that's something you can't escape from.

It can be terrifying, especially when you're taking over from someone else. Len, Bruno and I still get nervous – and they do two series in America every year as well as the UK show. Whatever it looks like, it isn't easy. Some people can do it and some people can't.

Darcey started really well but she had a few things to iron out, most notably her use of the word, 'Yah'. In Australia, where she's been living, they say 'yah' for 'yes' and she's picked that up but, when she first went on, people were finding that a little bit irritating, because she was saying it at the end of every sentence. She must have done about twenty 'yahs' a show for the first two weeks. There were some comments in the press about it and there was an influx of people emailing the BBC, saying, 'Does Darcey really have to say that many 'yahs'? I found it quite amusing, and endearing, because it sort of set her apart from the crowd, but it wasn't going down well.

On the judges' desk we each have a little pad, so we can scribble down the name and number of the couple dancing, and our thoughts, then there's space for our marks to go. I generally write three words that might remind me of something that happened through the routine, and that gives me the basis for my comments.

On week three of the series, I glanced over at Darcey's pad and, on every page, she had written, 'Don't say yah!' It was in huge print on the opposite side of the page so she could always see it, and remind herself not to say it. She managed to wean herself off the 'yahs' quite quickly though.

Darcey is amusing company backstage. Everyone thinks she's prim and proper but she's got a wicked sense of humour – and she farts! She's really down to earth, but she looks so elegant and poised that you can't imagine her backstage hoiking her leg up and blowing off. And burping. It's not that she's uncouth, but she's normal. She's like most dancers, in that they're free and easy with their body and used to hanging around a 'company', where everyone is like family. That's what I love about her.

She was so excited about the series and how it went and,

at the wrap party, she just wanted to let her hair down. She becomes the party girl and then has no inhibitions at all. She was up on the dance floor shaking it about to 'Dancing Queen', trying to dance with everybody. She was really up for a big one. She's adorable.

As the series progressed she got better and better and became a little bit more herself. At first, you do feel like you've got to put a persona on, but actually you shouldn't think like that. You should just be yourself, be honest and to the point. If you put on any airs and graces and pretence, the audience will spring that immediately, because *Strictly Come Dancing* judging is instantaneous, and you've got to react to what you're seeing in the moment. If I had preconceived semi-scripted ideas, they would invariably go out the window because you have no idea what you will see on that night, even if you've seen rehearsals clips. I watch *It Takes Two*, which is the only time I get to see a little bit of training, just to see what steps the couples might be doing, but that's the only information we have. Our critiques have to be spontaneous, so my biggest fear is that they come to me and say, 'Craig, what do you think about that?' and I go blank. It hasn't happened yet – but there's always a first time.

Luckily, as you may have guessed, I generally form an opinion pretty quickly.

Of course, freezing or stumbling over words isn't the only likely pitfall. As yet, I have never given a wrong score on the TV show, but I did screw up on the 2012 tour. I pushed the wrong button and immediately thought, 'Argh!' – I'd given one of the couples a four instead of a seven. The keypad we press to record our score is basically the same layout as a phone, and if you slip, it's easy to hit the four, instead of the seven – which is a huge difference. But I couldn't admit I had messed up, so I had to fudge it and slag off the dance more than I should have done!

There is always good and there's always bad in every dance routine, but I was preparing to give quite a nice appraisal until I saw the number '4' flashing and I thought, 'Oh. My. God. What am I going to say?' And then I had to revert to negative. It was a terrible moment. I didn't apologize or tell anyone at the time.

Fortunately, on tour the judges' scores don't matter, they are just for guidance. When it really matters, on the TV show, I'm *very* careful about what button I push. As soon as the dance has finished, we are required to push a number from one to ten on the electronic keypad on the desk, and once it's done, you can't change it. No one can see what anyone else is scoring, so we have to make an instant decision and, once you've hit the pad, that score goes to the gallery and then the gallery type it up to make all the numbers.

It's a nightmare if you hit the wrong button and don't realize it. It happened to Arlene, who once scored a six on the computer and then held up the 7 paddle,which was a bone of contention. The same thing happened to Bruno in the 2009 quarter finals, when Austin Healey was dancing. He pressed 10 and held up the 9 paddle. It's very easy to do, and – so far – my fumbling fingers have behaved themselves.

As a man known for voicing opinions, I'm quite a fan of Twitter, but it leaves me open to a lot of abuse, particularly from fans of the *Strictly* contestants I am judging. When Nicky Byrne started out, in series ten, the Westlife fans launched a torrent of tweets at me. They were going absolutely mad. But it wasn't until Hollywood Night, when he dressed as the Jim Carrey character, The Mask, for the quickstep that we saw him flourish. That meant I could be kinder to him, because he was actually putting some personality into it.

In the early weeks, he thought I had it in for him and he was a little bit down on me, backstage, although he knows it's a competition and he knows that I'm a different person there than I am when I'm judging. I wouldn't be harsh backstage like that. If he came up and wanted advice, I'd give it to him.

Some celebrities in each series are a little wary and, on that series, former England cricket captain Michael Vaughan was really cagey with me. He seemed a bit nervous of me and that was quite amusing. It is funny when you walk in to the star bar – the backstage area where the couples hang out and warm up – and suddenly the mood completely changes. They know that I'm going to be speaking my mind when we're on air and it makes them a little bit nervous, so they're not as chummy backstage. As I said earlier, when we go on tour the judges' scores don't count, so you can have a little bit more of a laugh with it and they get to banter back and change what they say every night. That keeps it fresh, but you also get to know them a little bit better.

Jerry Hall proved a bit of a dance dis-ah-ster. She just didn't try that hard, and she's no Giselle when it comes to dance. As a model, you might think she would know how to use her body to the best advantage but she's not really that capable. Our previous models, Lisa Snowden and Kelly Brook, were fabulous, but Jerry, hunched over Anton Du Beke, was a sight to behold. Backstage, however, I adored her. She has an amazingly dry sense of humour, absolutely brilliant, and she made me laugh all the time. A lot of the celebs say, after the show, 'Why did you have to say that about me? Why are you picking on me?' I always say, 'It's your dancing I'm commenting on, not you as a person, darling.' But Jerry didn't care one little bit and it was fantastic because she never once complained about something I'd said.

Johnny Ball, who was first out, was devastated when he didn't do well because he really wanted to get through and he loved it so much. Backstage, he was so full of enthusiasm and couldn't quite believe that he was out in the first week. And with his daughter Zoë being the *It Takes Two* presenter, and a brilliant past contestant, he wanted to do her proud and he didn't want to be the first one out on her sofa. It was a really sad state of affairs, but he was remaining positive throughout it, which I thought was champion of him.

Lisa Riley and Robin Windsor made a fantastic couple on the show – and they remain great friends now. That's the *Strictly* effect.

Apart from being slagged off by Nicky's fans on Twitter and the social networks, I was being accused of favouritism towards Lisa Riley, which was totally untrue. I don't have any favourites. I judge each contestant specifically on merit, on their dance routines, and Lisa was a very good dancer, as were Denise Van Outen and Kimberley Walsh. I don't mark them favourably just because I like them. I mark them favourably if I like their dancing.

Lisa was a wonderful surprise, because she had such enthusiasm and a passion for the dance and the experience, and I really loved that in her. She forged such a fantastic relationship with Robin Windsor, her dance partner, and now they are inseparable, best mates. It's wonderful to see that those relationships continue on in real life. It's not just that you finish the job and then you're done. *Strictly* changes people's lives for ever and dance partners forge incredible relationships. Robin was able to support her through the grief she was suffering over the death of her mum, whom she lost shortly before the series started. She had a really tough time dealing with it and coming back in the public eye in such a massive way and she was unable to grieve properly for her mum because she had to do *Strictly*, which takes up a hell of a lot of time. At the same time, it was probably a huge help, because it gave her something else to think about, and a really good reason to put her all into dancing well. That's why I loved her, because she'd come out and give everything a shot. Plus, she proved to be really, really talented.

Competition was fierce though. Denise van Outen was simply incredible. Her Egyptian Charleston will go down in *Strictly* history and her jive was equally spectacular. Kimberley was wonderful, a great dancer, and Dani Harmer was a real pocket rocket, a feisty little mover.

In the end, though, Louis Smith was a worthy winner. He wasn't entirely the judge's choice because there were better dancers but he was the people's choice, and that's the beauty of the show. It was Olympic year, and he was one of our finest Olympic athletes, so the audience were behind him. He's probably been one of our best rumba boys ever because he had the right hip action, which most of the men find really hard. Plus, he was entertaining, he's skill is very good looking, and he did a great job to get to the final and then win it.

Louis also managed to bag the most trophies on the 2013 tour, although Denise won a few and Lisa Riley was chuffed to bits when she topped the poll in her hometown of Manchester. Generally, on the tour, the person who won the TV competition doesn't win. Like Kara Tointon, who won the series, lost out almost every night to Matt Baker on tour, but the world was still backing our Olympic champ.

Phil Tufnell returned to the fold for this one and provided a bit of humour. His dancing had improved and he really went for it. It wasn't like his dancing was horrendous, he just made odd choices, especially with his hip movements. But the crowd loved him and he's such a great personality and a wonderful team member so he's brilliant to be on tour with.

This year was a great tour for me it all came together easily, no arguments or major obstacles to avoid, the producers and cast and I were getting along well and it was fun to rehearse because we had a new addition to the company in the form of a new choreographer, Jason Gilkison. He really made the job easy because his choreography was excellent and he is such a charming and funny man to work with. We hit it off instantly and the rehearsal process went smoothly. Also, I was in love again and feeling good about myself. I was planning my trip to Australia with Doctor D for my sister's wedding and had everything to look forward to. It was exciting, positive and a shorter run, which everyone was pleased about. Len and Bruno were even behaving! All too good to be true.

It was a tradition that Doctor D came up to London and went to the *Strictly* Halloween special. We'd spoken on occasion since the holiday but he had never explained why he had gone cold on me, so, when Halloween 2012 came around, he came up for the show, as a friend. And then, of course, we got together again.

'Oh, dear,' I thought. 'Third time round now. What am I doing?' But I'd been sane through the year because I'd been concentrating on myself and I felt I was in a much better position to have a relationship. Plus, this time we seemed to be on a more even keel, with him planning to see me more often and coming up with all these fantastic ideas of where we could meet and how we could get together.

'This is looking promising,' I thought, but I wasn't holding my breath, because twice bitten, twice shy. I was holding something in reserve.

Towards the end of the year, I booked the six-week trip back to Australia that I'd been promising the family all those years. My sister, Diane, had put off the wedding so I could be there, and she begged me to give her a date, so I couldn't let her down again. I told her the dates I would be free and she immediately started booking the venues and organizing the wedding so that, this time, I couldn't pull out. To prove to her that I was coming, I booked my travel ticket and paid for it, and then had to tell Doctor D, so I tried to play it cool.

'I'm going to Australia on 15 February,' I told him. 'I'll be there for six weeks. You're more than welcome to join me if you have the notion.'

'I'll get back to you on that,' he said. 'I need to check if I can get time off work.'

'Oh, no,' I thought. 'This could end in disaster, like the last time I asked him away on a holiday. Craig, what are you letting yourself in for?' I didn't want to lose him again because he's just gorgeous, the most divine man on earth.

I gave him the dates. I gave him my flight number and when I was returning, and then I left the ball in his court. A few days later, he sent me an email – with his own flight details! He'd actually booked it. He was actually coming!

He could only get four weeks off work, so we were flying out together and he would come back before me. 'You arrange the itinerary,' he said. 'But I wouldn't mind going to Sydney because I have a sister there.'

After that, the relationship went full steam ahead, but not so full-on as moving in with Grant or Lloyd, when we were never out of each other's pockets. This was an entirely different sort of relationship partly because he lives so far away, partly because he's older – forty – so he was more mature, more settled. He was used to living by himself, we had similar homes and a similar taste in everything and we just got on really, really well.

I was in a really good place because of my independence

and because I didn't need to rely on anyone, and actually I wasn't looking for anything. People say when you stop looking for love, it finds you, but I never quite believed that until I got that email, and booking confirmation and it put a massive smile on my face. Then I couldn't wait to book all the internal flights and get planning. I sent him an itinerary, which partly revolved round my sister's wedding. I was aware it was going to be a bit of an assault on him, meeting my entire family, all on the first day, but he seemed up for it.

Before we left, I wanted to establish where we were. 'Can I just ask one question?' I said. 'Are we in a relationship? Are you going to be sleeping with anyone else? Because I won't sleep with anyone else.'

'No, I won't sleep with anyone else,' he replied.

'Then we're in a relationship,' I said.

We were both a bit nervous about the holiday, because we had only ever spent three consecutive days together but the flight over put my mind at rest. We got on like a house on fire.

On the day we arrived, it was 36 degrees and, as it was the middle of winter in London, we were used to minus three. What a difference. We spent the first day meeting and greeting the immediate family at my sister Sue's house. We arrived at six in the morning and, by 9.30 a.m., we were drinking champagne round the pool. Then, at eleven o'clock that same morning, we had to rush off to the wedding rehearsal, so it was straight in at the deep end.

Di, my middle sister, was marrying Death Metal fanatic Dave Leight – giving her the moniker of Di Leight, which has already been commuted to 'D-Leight' as a running gag.

My father being too ill to attend, Di wanted me and my little brother Trent to give her away so I'd bought matching suits for us by Ted Baker from London with me, co-ordinated to match the other wedding outfits, and I took all those suits over. The whole family were at the wedding rehearsals – including my youngest niece, who's only one, and whom I had never seen before. Before I knew it, Doctor D was bottle-feeding her in the pew in at the rehearsal, which I found hilarious. Then he had to meet Death Metal Dave's side of the family.

Once we'd finished the rehearsal, in thirty-six-degree heat, we had a big family luncheon back at Sue's place then, in the evening, Trent's band, Mushroom Giant, were playing and he was really keen for us to come. The gig was in a pub called the Tote, which is famous as one of the last remaining places in Melbourne where bands can gig and it's all really heavy metal and dance trance, and everyone has dreadlocks. So after a full on day, with us getting off a plane at six, the wedding rehearsal and a boozy lunch, we were still up at midnight, watching my brother play drums, completely jet lagged. As soon as we got home we collapsed into bed, totally exhausted.

The wedding was a few days later, on 23 February. It was gorgeous and the weather was blazing hot. Di looked fantastic – D-Leight-ful in fact – and as I walked her down the aisle there were quite a few tears in the congregation.

The service was odd, but brilliant, because the guy who conducted the ceremony was a comedian who was the spitting image of *Doctor Who* star Tom Baker, wearing a pair of seventies flares. I've never seen anything quite like it.

Di was having her reception at home and, after the ceremony, Trent got back first and called me in a panic. 'Craig, you won't believe it!' he said. 'There are only nine bottles of white in the fridge.'

'You are joking!' I said. 'There are over a hundred people coming to this wedding!' So I had to make a detour and pick up loads of booze on the way. It turned out there was plenty more but they'd stashed it somewhere else and no one could find it, so it wasn't drunk.

The reception was set around the pool, with a beautiful marquee and, initially, it was very la-di-dah, gorgeous and classy. Then people started getting hot and stripping off and getting into the pool, so the whole thing ended up in all sorts of debauchery. It went from one extreme to the other and became a massive pool party with loads of heavy metal fans. I'd never seen so many Metallica T-shirts at a wedding reception. There were a lot of broken bottles, a lot of blood, a lot of people drunk diving into the pool breaking their noses, so it ended up spectacularly bad, but brilliant at the same time.

Doctor D treated me to one of the most romantic moments ever and was so very special, a balloon flight over Melbourne. It was my first balloon ride and was just stunning! We had to leave very early in the morning at 5 a.m. at a park in Melbourne and it was just amazing seeing all the balloons fill with hot air as the sun was rising, the short blasts of fire making them come to life and eventually rise into the cityscape. A truly irreplaceable memory of taking off and flying in silence over the tall skyscrapers was a sight to behold. The landing was even better as we had to stand backwards in the basket that held ten of us as we were dragged backwards along the ground until we stopped. Getting out of the basket at this angle was a real challenge, there was no way you could do this elegantly.

After a week in Melbourne, we went to Sydney to visit Doctor D's sister. I was quite excited to meet some of his family because I felt we were getting to know each other finally and our four weeks together would help to solidify the relationship. Then we joined Di up in Palm Cove, a beach resort in Cairns, on the Queensland coast so we could see the Barrier Reef. I flew my mum from Melbourne and she was a bit nervous because she never travelled alone before on a domestic flight. She'd only ever done international business, darling!

My sister had hired a big old place with a swimming pool, but Doctor D and I stayed at a fabulous hotel, Pepper's Beach Club, and spent the week with mum, Di, and Dave before heading to my hometown of Ballarat.

The Ballarat Begonia Festival was on at the time. The annual event holds some precious memories for me because I once won Best Fancy Dress Costume. I was around thirteen and dressed as a big fat clown in a costume made by my grandmother, with a hoop that created the enormous waistline. I applied my own make-up and danced and skipped the entire procession. There was a photo of me on the front page of the *Ballarat Courier* the following day, the same paper that I had to deliver to many houses as a paperboy. It was very exciting. I was also in the Ballarat Memorial Marching Band, and we performed at the Begonia Festival Parade every year. We arrived at Ballarat that weekend, and it was perfect timing because Doctor D got to see that unique event, then it was time for him to fly back.

Before we left for our trip, I had thought, 'Let's see how

we get on, we might hate one another by the end of it.' But now I was really sad to see him leave. I was trying not to show it, though, so I did what I call a 'dump and run' at the airport, where you just drop someone off and then drive off. I find that easier than going through the checkout system and hanging around and then the last you see of them is going through the double doors into oblivion. I prefer to say all my goodbyes in private before the airport run. I hate people coming into the airport with me and waiting around.

Just before I was due to go to Australia on my holiday, a very close friend of mine passed away unexpectedly. Her name was Cayte Williams, although she married a few years ago and her named changed to Finley, and she was just fifty when she died. We had known one another since the early nineties. We were the original 'Heartbreakers', sharing a house (which we dubbed the Heartbreak Hotel) in Camden Town with my best friend Clifford, Lloyd and me. We had some amazing times in that house over the five years we shared it. Cayte's nickname was Shaggles and we all got on so well, those years went extremely fast.

I was at the Liverpool arena, on the *Strictly* tour, when I received the call saying that Cayte had been suddenly rushed into hospital. She hadn't been feeling well on the Saturday three days before the call, so had gone to A&E to get checked out. They had kept her in hospital, but as I was in Liverpool I couldn't get there straight away, so I thought I'd go and see her when I got back to London, never thinking for one moment it was going to be a life-threatening blood disorder. I received this email from my friend Pilch on 28 January:

> *Dear All*
>
> *For those of you who do not already know, I am sorry to tell you that Cayte is not at all well. She was taken in to Whipps Cross Hospital on Saturday and is being moved to University College Hospital.*
>
> *It is thought she has thrombotic thrombocytopenic purpura (TTP) which is an autoimmune disease producing tiny blood clots throughout the body and causing damage to the red blood cells and organs. As far as I can work out it is a very serious illness but the prognosis is good if treatment is prompt. Treatment will involve 'cleaning' her blood plasma.*
>
> *I have not seen her and do not yet know if visiting is possible. Her sister, Liz, is with her and in touch with me and Sharanne. Bill and Charley are with her too.*
>
> *I will email you all again when I have more*

*information.*

   *Lots of love*

   *Pilch*

I replied at 8:43 the following morning as I didn't get my emails till then:

*Thanks, Pilch, for letting me know, please keep me informed. I'm away on tour at the moment up in Liverpool but if there is anything I can do don't hesitate, darling. x*

*Craig*

At 09:40 that very same morning I received a call from my ex-wife Jane, who was great friends with Cayte, telling me that Cayte was dead. I just couldn't believe it. I went into total shock. My first reaction to Jane was, 'You're joking?!' which is pretty stupid. Why would Jane joke about something like that? It was just panic. My thoughts turned immediately to her gorgeous son Charley and her fabulous husband Bill. OMG, how? Why? It can't be true? Random thoughts were rocketing through my mind and I was stuck in limbo in Liverpool, feeling a sense of helplessness.

I had a short conversation with Jane, and agreed that,

as she was so upset, I would call all our close-knit circle of friends and break the news. As I phoned the people that needed to know, all of them said exactly the same thing, 'You're joking?!' It was a difficult, heartbreaking task, as we were all so close, almost like family. I had taken us all on an amazing holiday reunion to the Lighthouse on Lundy Island the previous year, a place where we had shared a mad fun-packed break back when we were penniless, young and free. We'd also had a photo-book launch party of the holiday, that Cayte attended on 4 November 2012, just months before, so none of us could get our heads around the whole thing.

The funeral was being held the very day I was flying out to Australia for my sister's wedding, so I was so really worried that I was going to have to miss it. As it happened, I was able to be a coffin bearer and attend the service but unfortunately I couldn't go on to the wake and I so wanted to be there for everyone else. It was so very sad.

Sometimes life just doesn't seem fair. She was one of the nicest, warmest, generous, highly entertaining people I've ever met and had the pleasure of being friends with as well as being a quick witted, intelligent, talented and gifted writer.

The following interview was from the Lundy Island photo book and will give you a very small indication of her wonderful sense of humour. We all love dressing up as different characters and Lundy Island was no exception to the rule. She named me Miss Lundy on one particular evening and then got creative with a pretend interview, all of which was based on a hint of truth and actually what happened during our stay there. My dear friend Wendy Olver did the artwork, which was amazing.

*Interview with Miss Lundy in **Island Life** magazine, 19 August 2011.*

*Meeting Miss Lundy is like meeting a legend. In her heyday, she was the most beautiful woman in the Bristol Channel and now, twenty-two years later, she's still as gorgeous as ever.*

*Admittedly, the luscious blonde locks have been replaced by a swathe of smooth silver hair: the entertaining – some would say tawdry – frocks have been usurped by comfortable walking pants and a subtle fleece. But she still has the cheekbones and long limbs of a sleek Lundy Island pony.*

*'How lovely to meet you,' she breathes as she welcomes me into her lighthouse keeper's cottage. 'I love this island,' she says, dreamily, as she inhales the salty air. 'It's where I was brought up and wore my first see-*

*through Moroccan dress over a black leotard.'*

*No one really knows Miss Lundy's past. One day she just appeared, at the age of seven, in the Marisco Tavern, pulling pints for the locals and tap dancing on tables for thruppence. Looked after by Floss and Moll, then ladies of the Tavern, she grew into a beautiful woman and was always happy to offer extra service to island visitors. She certainly made her mark on the Landmark Trust.*

*Miss Lundy was crowned in 1989. She entered the first, and only, year of the beauty pageant and wowed the judges – Blind Bill, the tavern's odd job man and 'Mobility Scooter' Steve – who said they'd have voted for her as the winner even if there had been other contestants.*

*She came out on the cover of* Island Life *magazine, all blonde hair and pouting lips. Who can forget that striking pose of her bending over and yelling pleasantries out of her window at passing hikers? What an ambassador for this lovely land! Or her picnic walks – red letter days in the Lundy Island calendar – she'd gracefully walk a full 200 yards before settling nicely into a wind-sheltered grotto to crack open a bladder of wine. The way she navigated rabbit warrens in six-inch heels has been a benchmark for island women since.*

*But the island could never contain her, and Miss*

*Lundy went on to travel the world as a dancer. She introduced the continents to the TrotFox, the indigenous Lundy Island dance. She won fans all over the world, from the Lido in Paris to Le Chat Noir in the bohemian backstreets of North London. She has fans all over the world.*

*But all through the glamorous times, she never forgot her home. At the height of her fame, she was the cover star of* Time *magazine, where she cuddled two Lundy Island Puffins, nestled sweetly in the makeshift hammocks of her black lace bra. 'I still foster Lundy wildlife to this day,' she smiles. 'I have a Manx shearwater stuffed in my knickers.'*

*It was while in Austria on tour that she met the love of her life, Count Coch. For years she lived in a mansion in Vienna 'living the highlife, darling' and now she's back. 'I'm so glad to be home,' she smiles sweetly and knocks back a vodka. 'I want the quiet life now.'*

*Still as fit and lithe as ever, she has replaced dancing for another form of exercise, and is an avid climber of this beautiful island – and quite a social one at that. 'I'm a member of a climbing club,' says the sprightly forty-something, 'but some two-bit TV celebrity accused me of being a lesbian, just because we were all women in our club. Fame, darling. It's not what it used to be!'*

*And with that, she tosses her hair and staggers into*
*the blustery night, fighting the breeze and hiccupping.*
*Some habits, however delicious, never die ...*

As you can see, she was wonderful to be around and I love and miss her terribly. RIP my beautiful friend.

On another sad occasion my good friend Gow Hunter slipped away from us all. He'd been suffering for a long time with ill health. The last time I saw him and was properly able to chat to him was at the hospice in June 2011. He was in fantastic spirits and planning a big party, for which he was hoping he would be out of hospital, but sadly that was never to be. The next time I went to see him was to be in his final hours, and I could only hold his hand and kiss him gently on the forehead. His breathing was intermittent and shallow. I'm so glad I was able to get that time with him and can't thank his family enough for giving me that privilege. He died – aged just fifty-one – on 30 June 2011.

An actor, dancer and choreographer, Gow had featured in Kate Bush's 1986 video for her 'Hounds of Love' single. He trained in classical ballet, danced with various ballet companies and continued with diverse and challenging work in television, video, film, theatre and opera. He was very fortunate to live and work in many different countries – Paris, Rome, Geneva, Seoul and London to name but a few – and to work with very talented performers/directors such as Kate Bush, Placido Domingo, David Bailey and Robert Lepage.

After a successful career as a professional dancer, Gow was accepted into Central Saint Martin's School of Art and Design, where he completed a degree in Textile Design. He was so excited about it and we would have meetings about potentially using his creations in my shows. His designs have been seen on the catwalks of London Fashion week, solo exhibitions and in his own label of knitted textile accessories.

Gow always had a passion for anything creative and photography had always been one of his most inspiring pastimes. After moving to Tokyo in 2007 he spent much of his time taking pictures of Japan and was just beginning to realize his lifetime passion for photography. I have all his books and they are incredible. Such a terrible loss to the world but his memory and books will live on for ever.

With my handsome travelling companion gone, I spent my last two weeks just seeing more of the family, including my sister Mel, whose drinking was getting out of hand.

I had known Mel had a drink problem for a while. Back in 2007, when I was judging on *Dancing With the Stars* in New Zealand, she flew over from Melbourne to stay with me in Wellington, and Trent came out a couple of days later. She had been off the drink for three weeks but she gets scared on aeroplanes so she had about five whiskies and, when she arrived, she was already a bit tipsy. She'd also bought a bottle of Wild Turkey in the duty-free and she managed to drink about half that before we went out for dinner.

We'd been invited out by Erina Malloy, the producer of the show, and Debra Kelleher, who is the executive producer, to a lovely restaurant called Caio. By the time we arrived, Mel was getting loud and lairy and becoming slightly embarrassing. In the restaurant, she lost control completely. As soon as the wine arrived at the table, she was grabbing the bottle and necking it; she was trying to light up cigarettes where it's illegal to smoke, which is just about everywhere in New Zealand; she kept slapping the waiter on the bum and screaming profanities at the table, and I was getting really annoyed. I kept hissing, 'Mel! You've got to stop!'

Erina and Debs were being really good and putting up with it, trying to calm her down, as was my friend Nelson, who had also come to visit. When the food arrived, Mel leaned over Erina's plate, stretched her arm out and just grabbed a handful and then shoved it in her face, chomped on it in a drunken daze, and then spat it back out in to her hand. Then, horror of horrors, she put it back on Erina's plate.

The execs from TVNZ were in a state of shock and I was furious. I said, 'Erina, I'm so sorry! Mel – get outside!' I took her out to have a chat with her and told her she had to calm down, then she started crying and eventually we went back in. As we sat down, she said, 'It's all fine now, isn't it, Craig?' in a really obnoxious manner. Soon after that, Debs took her out on to a balcony so she could have a fag and, fifteen minutes, later they came back. Mel took the place next to Debs rather than sit with me. For four or five minutes everything seemed calmer, then Mel took the bottle of wine, filled a wine glass, looked at Debs and then slowly poured the whole glass over Debs' head. We had no choice but to leave the restaurant and it was still only 9 p.m.!

The day after that awful episode, Mel didn't even remember most of what she'd done, but we were going to the opening of *Swan Lake* and Debs and Erina and everyone from TVNZ was going to be there. I said, 'You have got to apologize to these people – and don't you dare drink tonight.' She behaved herself that night but, on the final night, she fell backwards off a stool after the show and, when we left, I refused to walk out with her. Trent was there by this time, trying to look after her, and he said, 'I've got to do this all the time. I'm glad you've seen this side of it.'

I hadn't seen much of her since then, other than the six weeks she spent with me in London and on our holiday with Nikki. But her drinking worried me then and I had reports from home about her behaviour.

Happily, she had been reasonably well behaved at the wedding. She had a drink but she wasn't out of hand. Then, on Good Friday, the day before I was due to leave Australia, Sue threw a 'last supper' for the family, and Mel turned up absolutely slaughtered, and then embarrassed herself, once again, with totally inappropriate behaviour. I Left Australia feeling horribly worried about her because we had been through so many alcohol issues with my dad.

The problem with alcoholism is that it has an impact on the people that love you so I was worried for Mel but also for Mum, who lived through alcoholism and its awful consequences all her life with my father. When we were growing up, Dad was a loving man when sober, and an angry, violent one when drunk, which was a lot of the time. He is still an alcoholic and now can't survive without the booze. According to the doctors, if he was not to drink for one day, his system would close down and he would die, so, ironically, it's the alcohol that's keeping him alive at the moment. He's just been through three operations, one after the other – a hip replacement, a tumour removed from his face and an enormous amount of skin cancer from his chest, so he's been in the wars, and he has to drink through it, to the point of having to have six tinnies a day at the hospital. They had to let him drink, otherwise he wouldn't survive.

People don't realize what alcohol can do to you, if it gets out of control like that, and we just don't want to see my sister slide down the same slippery slope, which is so easy to do if you're the son or the daughter of an alcoholic.

Mel's got a new boyfriend, who I hope will be able to look after her. It used to be my brother, Trent, who told me he'd been looking after her for years, and making sure she gets home safely but we can't keep enabling her.

I hope she does get help and tackle the problem, because I do love her dearly and I want to see the old Mel back. I want to see the happy, vivacious, outgoing, fun-loving, delicious girl that she is. We get flashes of her on occasion, but unfortunately, due to alcohol and alcoholism, she can be something of a Jekyll and Hyde.

Doctor D's intolerance to my fame became majorly apparent when he planned a weekend away for us and a visit to meet his mum in Hereford. Well this was to prove to be the beginning of the end. Hereford is a relatively small town so when we went for a walk in the town the *Strictly* fans were out in force so we were continually stopped for photos and autographs, everything he hated. I went in to Boots on the high street as some shampoo I love was on special offer and I'd run out. I was recognized immediately and then suddenly people were queuing for photos and autographs. His mum loved the attention but Doctor D was feeling very uncomfortable, as people would come up to him and ask him to take the photos. We couldn't go anywhere without this occurring and I felt him becoming increasingly distant. This was to be the spanner in our relationship.

Indeed, it proved not to be third-time lucky, sadly, with Doctor D. A couple of months after our Australian trip, in May 2013, we took another quick break in Tenerife, but things didn't go quite so swimmingly as they had down under.

He had been acting distant for a few weeks and, at the resort, his mind seemed to be elsewhere. Eventually, I broached the subject of us to find out what was wrong. This time, he gave me a full explanation, which boiled down to the fact that he was uncomfortable with my 'celebrity status' and, while he loved being with me in private, he didn't like going out in public because I'd be recognized and people would want to talk to me and get pictured with me.

I was sad, of course, but I totally understand why my lifestyle might scare someone off. Not everyone wants to be thrust into the limelight, just because the person they choose to be with is famous, but I can't change the fact that my face is familiar to millions of people. The irony is that one of the things I loved about him was that he didn't care about the showbiz parties, the glitz and glamour of the job, and meeting famous people, like some others who express an interest in me for all the wrong reasons.

Fame does have many perks but making it easy to have a relationship is not one of them.

# CHAPTER 9

# TIME TAKES ITS TOLL

Ann was back as my Widdy in Waiting when we opened the panto in High Wycombe in 2012. We had a brilliant time with a really fantastic cast, as we have every year and Ann and I had some funny times on stage. In one show, I dried when Ann was on and I could not think of my next line at all. I was just stood there and Ann saved the day, because she knew all my lines better than she knew her own.

When you do two shows a day, you don't know what act you're in sometimes. You think, 'Have I done the first act or am I in the second act now? What speech is this?' It gets a bit confusing and I just completely blanked.

'Do you know, Widdy,' I said. 'I've completely forgotten what I'm meant to say next.' Of course, the audience roared with laughter, but it was true, I'd completely lost my train of thought.

Ann said, 'Oh, I think it's something about being angry with me,'

'Ah, yes, that's right,' I said, gratefully. 'I'm very angry with you Widdy. You have let Princess Snow White out of your sight and we don't know where to find her!' It was hilarious.

The audience make the panto fun for me, because I sometimes feel like I'm a little bit imprisoned. My dressing room in High Wycombe had no windows and once I have walked into the building I'm in drag for eight hours, from midday all the way through to ten o'clock at night. I have to do a physical warm up, a vocal warm up, get the slap on, get all the stuff on and then I can't take it off, meaning I can't go outside at all between shows so I have food brought in. I eat at five o'clock and then sleep between five thirty and six thirty, for an hour, in full drag, before the seven o'clock show.

I'm a sight, I'm telling you, lying down for a kip in full drag. It's tragic! Plus, it's painful. My legs are killing me, my hips are killing me, the balls of my feet are screaming from prancing around in high heels, and all you want to do is go to bed, but then you've got to get up and do another show. The corset is really tight as well, meaning I have very shallow breathing because it cinches me in so much that it crushes my ribs, but to breathe in order to sing and dance, you need deep breathes through the back. So it's quite a painful experience for the whole month. I always get nervous when October's coming round, as soon as *Strictly* starts, because then I know that the panto is looming. Sometimes, to be honest, it was a relief to do *Strictly* on Saturday nights because I could sit down and judge rather than having to be spinning, tangoing and cha-cha-cha-ing in my six-inch heels.

Having said all that, it's fabulous fun and I really enjoy it. I'm glad that fear factor has gone away. When I first started my panto stints, I kept thinking back to the time when, as a young man, I was touring with Danny La Rue, and I got such bad stage fright I fluffed up my lines every night. I was terrified it would happen again, but in panto you can get away with it to a certain extent and make it amusing. And if you make a right royal cock-up, the audience love it anyway because they've seen Craig Revel Horwood screw up.

Because of my commitment to *Strictly*, the theatres 'go dark' on the Saturday, which should be the big money-spinner evening, but we still pack them out on Sundays and the rest of the week. Because the show is topical and because they're seeing me in drag and they don't know me for that, really, it's great. Some of the kids don't recognize it's me at all, because I never de-mask, and I try play the queen as a proper woman – albeit the truck-driving diesel-guzzling type of woman. I'm not as ultra fem as I could be, but that's not the point of panto.

What I love most of all is the audience. They're up for a laugh, it's Christmastime, and not only do the kids love it, the adults love it because there's a lot of adult humour that goes over the kids' heads, which is funny in itself. It's the audiences that make me laugh as well. They crack me up when they shout out funny things. After every dance, everyone gives me a score. Sometimes it's a Len-style 'Seven', but mostly it's the lowest score they can possibly muster. People even bring in their own score cards, so it's all tongue in cheek and it gives me a chance to laugh at myself, which is important. I do it to not only prove that I'm a human being, but because I love performing, I love doing funny stuff and I have been thrilled to bring Lavish back from the dead, albeit disguised as The Wicked Queen – the most aptly named part I've ever played.

High Wycombe was the first time I directed the show as well as starring in it and, I have to admit, it proved too much for me. There was an enormous amount of pressure and strain, all at the same time as doing *Strictly* on a Saturday night. In future, I've decided to bow out of the direction side and just perform, which is so much easier because then I can just concentrate on myself rather than the whole company, the lighting and the choreography etc. I felt like I'd lost a little bit of my own performance because I was giving so much of myself to the other performers – and I felt too much like a control freak.

This year, coming I'm just starring and Lisa Riley will be joining me, in the Ann Widdecombe part, so the script will be different, but it will still be a lot of fun. The Ann and Craig Show had to come to an end, sadly, because you can only run the gags for so long and then you want to change the scenery. Ann was fantastic and I know she was really disappointed not to be doing it again this year. But casts are changing all the time, and it's important to keep the show fresh.

Three years ago, during my Crawley run of *Snow White and the Seven Dwarves*, I had noticed a dull ache in my both hips, which was worse on my right side. Injuries are a fact of every dancer's life. You have to work through tiredness, you have to work through injury, you have to work through all sorts of things and I would train with them for eight hours a day before performing in the evening. You tell yourself, 'I'll just finish this run and then rest.' But injury creates injury, and ignoring them can make things worse.

The worst one I had as a young man was when I was sixteen, and I was just starting out. I was performing in my second show *Rockin' the Town,* and I'd been given my first starring dance role, but it just pushed me to the limits and my body wasn't really ready for it so an existing hamstring injury got much worse, and I had a nine-month recovery period after that.

Since then I'd had twinges but nothing serious. Then in High Wycombe, last year, when I was dancing with Widdy, my right hip got much worse and I ended up limping about on stage – still wearing my high heels.

The horror and truth of it is that I had put my hip out completely and it was out of its socket for the whole of the panto run. I started popping painkillers, because I didn't know what else to do. I can't just stop doing panto in the middle of the season. As I said, you have to work through injury and generally it fixes, but as you get older your body takes longer to repair, and this is always an alarming concern.

To try to fix the problem, I had a massage every second day without fail; an osteopath came over at six in the morning and gave me a three-hour body massage; I'd do a proper warm-up. I did everything in my power to make it better, but it just wasn't getting better. I had to face the fact that I'd really done something dramatic here.

It was years of this sort of thing that caused my hip problems – but there's no use complaining: get it fixed and move on!

The initial problem then led to twinging all through my ligaments and it was extremely painful to the point where my hip was clicking and it was as much as I could do to drag myself across the stage. I was given really strong painkillers just to get me through it, and in my head I thought it would all work out fine because I'd got the *Strictly* the tour coming up, and I'd be able to rest through that, because I'd just be sitting at the desk. But it turns out that walking is the worst thing for it, so having to walk across arenas, every single day was making it worse.

Still assuming it was ligament damage and nothing to do with bone, I thought it would be fine after a good rest. Ligaments take up to six weeks to heal, as most dancers know, and you can tell the difference between a ligament and a muscle when you're a professional, but most dancers have injuries and most dancers think they're going to get better.

On any week of *Strictly*, there can be loads of people with injuries, and they'd have to just work through them, as every athlete does. So that's not a big deal, footballers do it, rugby players do it, so do dancers – your body is like an athlete's body, you know you've got to treat it as such.

Anyway, by the time the *Strictly* tour was over, I knew something was really wrong, so I went to see a specialist and had an MRI scan. I've never had an MRI scan before but I decided I needed one because it shows up everything, every little gory detail of what you've ever done to yourself in the past and what effect it's had on your body.

I was slightly concerned, because I had heard the scan wasn't very nice, but I went to see a doctor, who thought it was probably ligament damage and then told me the second possibility was that it was something to do with the joint. The worst scenario would be that it was hereditary and was something to do with arthritis. After the consultation, she sent me, straight away, for X-rays to make sure there were no fractures, and then for the scan.

As anyone who has had an MRI scan knows, it's not a pleasant experience. You're told not to move an inch, which is much harder than you might imagine. I thought I'd be able to relax, but you can't. It's frightening and, if you're claustrophobic, it's a nightmare.

They strap you down so you can't move, then tell you that even just one little twitch will blur the picture. Your hips are locked in, your ankles are strapped down, Then they put earphones on you and play music, to try to relax you, but as a dancer I hear the music and my toes start tapping or my muscles start twitching. It's a vicious circle. I'm supposed to lie still, I'm listening to music I love, I start twitching and then all the images blur and it takes even longer. You are in there for an hour already, and that's long enough.

The tube is really close to your face and the noise is frighteningly loud – like a jackhammer in your ear. So you are trying to hear the music over the top of a deafening racket, and trying to relax and they're talking to you, through the earphones, saying, 'Relax, don't move', but the more you think about not moving, the more your muscles and toes want to dance by themselves and you're trying to tell them, 'Don't do it!' It was horrible.

They scanned my hip area and my knees, which are buggered because of the dodgy hip. I asked the nurse, 'Can you do a whole body one?' I rather liked the idea of having a world map of my body. I thought it was like a photocopying machine and you'd pass through it and out the other end, and you would have a whole body image. But there's a camera that goes all the way around and that gives them different angles. I'd never been in one of these machines before and it's a torture device. Some people are into that, I'm not. It really was quite peculiar!

When it was over, a huge flood of relief came over me and I was so glad to get out. That was on a Thursday and I was asked to come back for the results on the following Monday. I spent a nail-biting weekend worrying, but I tried to put it out of my mind because, deep down, I knew what was wrong.

On Monday morning, I went to see the specialist and my MRI picture was plastered over a huge 55-inch high-definition TV. She was going through each X-ray and each MRI scan. I hadn't seen anything like them before, and I found it fascinating – you could see absolutely everything. Because it was my pelvis that was scanned, you can see all your bits and pieces, the crown jewels are all on display – inside out! – you can zoom in and see your hip.

I was early to the consultation but the doctor was running behind because one of her previous clients was late, so I was a little bit anxious; but she welcomed me in with a jolly smile, and I went in happy. I felt like I could walk properly, although it twinged occasionally and the painkillers had been masking it for months. As soon as I sat down, she said, 'It's the worst-case scenario: you've got arthritis, just like your family.' Then came the killer blow.

'And you need a hip-replacement.' A hip-replacement! Can you believe it? I was only forty-eight! The doctor told me it happens a lot to sportsmen and -women and, basically, I'd worn out both joints, from dancing and ballet, turning and forcing my hip joints out and then lodging them in the wrong place and it's just completely rubbed away. That is made worse by the fact that I have arthritis. My mother suffers from rheumatoid arthritis, but this is osteoarthritis. Ironically, I am patron of the National Osteoporosis Society – which is all about keeping bones healthy.

I've spent years preaching about preventing osteoporosis by exercising and now I discover that I'm one of the victims, because of *too much* exercise. One thing that didn't help was the fact that I was once anorexic, because then you have malnutrition of the bones, coupled with the dancing, and that makes it worse. My mixed-up past has come back and bitten me in the ass, once again.

But the beauty is, nowadays, you can be fixed, and these titanium hips are bloody amazing. I'd like to have a double one, to get it over and done with, but I think you've got to limp around on one while the new one recovers. I didn't know really how serious the operation was until I saw it online and I thought, 'Oh, my God!' I really shouldn't have looked.

I used to say to my mum, 'I bet I end up like you, after all my years of dancing.' And as it turns out, at forty-eight, I have. I'm going through something that really should have happened to me at seventy, not at my age. It's ghastly. The funny thing is, my mother had her hip done ten years ago, and my father has only just had his done in the last year – and he's seventy-two. But then he didn't do the physical exercise that I do, because he wasn't dancing for a living.

So many dancers have suffered this way. Darcey Bussell suffered crumbling hip bones and excruciating pain after years of ballet, and Gillian Lynne, who choreographed *Cats*, has had a double hip-replacement. She can still get her leg up and above her head, though.

So, I need to have a new titanium hip. I'm going to be

the bionic drag queen. The op means three months off work plus a month to build the muscle around it, so that the new hip doesn't pop out of place. I go to the gym already and I've been told you've got to keep exercising, and keep the muscle around it solid. There's an enormous amount of preparation for it, and there will be a great deal of physiotherapy before I do it, and afterwards. It'll be like doing ballet class again.

Having found that out in May 2013, I had to delay the surgery until February the following year, so it will be done as soon as I finish *Strictly* and the live tour. The doctor wanted me to have it done immediately, but I was in the middle of rehearsals for my new touring show, *Strictly Confidential* – and the show must go on. I couldn't just stop everything for three months, there's too much money at stake – not my money, but the considerable amounts that have been ploughed into the show, and that people need to make back – and there are many of people's careers to consider. I can't just bow out because I need a hip replacement.

In the meantime, I'm having cortisone injections into the ligament to get me through panto. They're giving me three injections into the hip joint just to numb it, but I'm doing more and more damage, until I finally get the bone chopped off and replaced with a titanium one. The new hip, I'm told, should last about ten years, but my left hip might need replacing in two years.

It's going to be interesting when I go through airport security in future. With a steel hip inside me, I'm going to be stopped every time I go through the body scanner, which is most embarrassing, but if it makes my hip work better then fantastic. I get stopped all the time anyway. If they recognize me they sometimes stop me just for a laugh, I'm sure of it. No bleeper goes off and still they shout, 'Oi, you, over here.' Then everyone comes over and has a look, they make me take my shoes off, then they run the shoes through the scanner and, because I have a tendency to go for fabulously flamboyant footwear, they have a laugh about the shoes. But really they usually just want a chat about *Strictly*.

*Strictly* fans have seen me dressed as the Tin Man, for Hollywood night, on the last series. Who knew then that by the time the surgeons have finished with me, I really will be the Tin Man. Altogether now – 'If I only had a heart!'

# CHAPTER 10

# CROCODILES EVERYWHERE

Since becoming a *Strictly* judge, I have been offered all sorts of TV work, from documentaries to game shows. Sometimes I think I've been on just about every show on the telly – although you won't catch me eating witchety grubs in the jungle any time soon.

One of my favourite regular gigs is *The Wright Stuff* with Matthew Wright on Channel Five. It's a great daytime magazine-type show and it gives me a chance to be myself and discuss a huge variety of topics – some of which I know nothing about and on some of which, unsurprisingly, I have a strong opinion. I'm generally never at a loss for words and that's probably why the producers invite me on the show so often. It's a good chance for the viewers to see me as me and not just the nasty judge from *Strictly*, and I love the banter about the various different subjects. I do, however, put my foot in it on occasion.

The show always begins with a meet-and-greet and a short discussion about what each of the panellists is up to or promoting. Each week, there are two resident celebrity panellists and one celeb who's promoting their book, theatre show or movie. It's always very interesting chatting to the new panellist each morning as we study the newspapers. It's quite an early call – for me anyway – as I have to be there at seven o'clock and then there's an awful lot of reading before we go on, so that we are clued up and have an opinion on all the stories that are in the news that day.

You have to read the news aloud, so the first time I did the show I was really nervous. I panicked about pronunciation of difficult words, places and names and, once, I got a bit flustered talking about MI5: when I read the headline out loud, I pronounced it as 'M-fifteen'! What motorway is that? I hear you asking. I was mortified when Matthew Wright quite clearly corrected me. But the news bit is definitely not an easy thing to do, as some of the other celebs that have come on have found out, too. You have to be able to put the news items in a bundle with an opinion but make sure you get all the interesting details and facts of the story across without making false statements or accusations. For instance, if you're talking about someone who's been accused of burglary, you can't say they did it and always have to use the word 'allegedly'. An *alleged* burglar is someone who has been accused of being a burglar but against whom no charges have been proved. An *alleged* incident is an event that is said to have taken place but has not yet been verified. In their zeal to protect the rights of the accused, newspapers and law-enforcement officials sometimes misuse *alleged*. Someone arrested for murder may be only an *alleged* murderer, for example, but is a real, not an *alleged*, suspect, in that his or her status as a suspect is not in doubt. Similarly, if the money from a safe is known to have been stolen and not merely mislaid, then we may safely speak of a theft without having to qualify our description with *alleged*.

As you can appreciate, it is a legal minefield and one must tread very carefully when interpreting news items. I have learned some valuable lessons along the way. I was once reading a story from the paper about travellers and used an unfavorable slang term – and paid a huge price for it. I was immediately truly sorry I had said it and I made a public apology for it at the time.

The same goes for religion, you have to be very careful not to upset people from various religious groups with your own beliefs. I once joked about Mary Magdalene being a prostitute, as an off-the-cuff remark, and all hell broke loose. It upset and offended many of the viewers, which I completely understood and, quite rightly, I was made to make a public apology. It is almost universally agreed today that characterizations of Mary Magdalene as a repentant prostitute are completely unfounded, yet, in my defence, for many centuries the Western (Catholic) church apparently taught that she was the person mentioned in the Gospels as being both Mary of Bethany and the 'sinful woman' who anoints Jesus in the Gospel of Luke. The notion of Mary Magdalene being a repentant prostitute has been prevalent over the centuries, from Ephraim the Syrian in the fourth century, Pope Gregory the Great in the sixth century and many artists, writers and Scripture commentators who followed their lead. Also, her story remains a subplot in Andrew Lloyd Webber's *Jesus Christ Superstar*, which I had performed in.

As you can see, you have to be somewhat guarded in what you say, and that's what makes the show so difficult. On the other hand, you can have fun with some stories. On one show, I had to talk about a man who was 'allegedly' eaten by a crocodile in Australia and the reason they thought a human had been eaten was because of 'the skid marks' the body left in the mud. A play on words always makes everyone laugh. The story itself was a tragic one, if it were true, but, perhaps inappropriately, you can often see the funny side.

Other shows have provided many a funny moment. I was asked to be a guest on *Celebrity Juice* in season five, alongside Johnny Vegas and Patsy Kensit. I was slightly concerned I wouldn't be funny enough, as I'm not a comedian by trade and that show was *so* off the wall and aimed at a very different audience to the *Strictly* fans. I went into the recording armed with the knowledge that I was to play the stooge and have every put-down and laugh enjoyed at my expense. I'm completely up for having the piss taken out of me and I actually quite enjoy it in a sadistic kind of way. I was placed on the panel next to the team captain, Fearne Cotton, and regular panelist, Rufus Hound. On the opposite side were Patsy, the other team captain, Holly Willoughby and Johnny Vegas. In the centre, of course, was the hilarious Keith Lemon (real name Leigh Francis). I'd never met 'Keith' before and to be honest was a little bit scared by him. His character is so outrageous – how was I to compete with the likes of him and all these bold personalities and comedy-gold geniuses? I felt completely out of my depth. The pressure to be funny was enormous so I had a good talk to myself and thought, 'Craig … just be yourself and let them take the lead.'

The show is edited down to forty-five minutes but it's filmed with a live studio audience – and that goes on for about four hours. On arrival, there's a briefing from the producers in the dressing room, so you understand what is required of you and how each section of the show will work. Some things they don't tell you, in order to surprise you and to get an honest first reaction. When I first met Keith backstage it was with trepidation; I didn't think I'd be able to understand him because he has a seriously thick Yorkshire accent and I thought he would be taking the piss out of me from the get-go. However, I couldn't have been more wrong; he was charming and his accent wasn't as thick as he portrays it in character. I have to confess, I thought Keith Lemon was really his name! I wasn't aware at the time that 'Keith' was one of Leigh's many characters.

In a 2006 interview with the *Guardian*, Leigh Francis claimed that Keith Lemon is loosely based on his best friend (whose name is Keith Lemon) and easily distinguished by his accent, bleached hair, ginger moustache and fake tan. According to Leigh, Lemon's background is that of a failed businessman, who was most successful in 1993, when he won the prestigious Businessman of the Year Award for his innovative creation, the 'securi-pole'. He has admitted that he hates the fake moustache that he has to wear while in character and removes it 'as soon as filming is finished'.

It's bizarre how the character has morphed into a blur of reality. Backstage, I didn't know whether to call him Keith or Leigh, so it was quite strange. I think I called him Keith the whole time. But the show was a blast to film and I really got into it. I didn't think I was very funny during the evening and I had a bit of an anxious moment afterwards, thinking, 'Why did I ever take the job? I'll come out of this one badly.' My fears were fuelled when Grant, still my boyfriend at the time, said that it wasn't my finest hour but, when I watched back the edit, I came across OK and, to my surprise, was quite funny. Thank God for creative editing!

About halfway through the filming, we were served a plastic pint of wine, which had been stored under the desk. That loosened my tongue and at the end I did a mad dance with Keith where I had to be Ricky Martin. I was really chuffed to have been asked – and with the way it turned out. Plus, it gave me a bit more confidence for when I'm working with comedians.

And it turns out that even a bunch of kids can make sure the joke is on me. In 2010, I was invited to do a CBBC show called *Robostar*. It was a new challenge-based series that gives CBBC viewers the chance to control a celebrity for a day. It's billed as a 'factual entertainment' series that turns stars into robots, and, in each episode, three best friends take total control of a celebrity, and must guide them through a series of top-secret, hilarious – and embarrassing – challenges. Every time the celeb passes a challenge the team wins a prize. The kids are totally in charge and the members of the public that get stung in the programme have no idea that the celebrity must obey the kids' every command.

At *Robostar* HQ, the presenters – JK and Joel (real names Jason King and Joel Ross) a cheeky double act I've worked with before on another CBBC show, *Hider in the House* – make the challenges harder and harder, and unleash the celebrity 'robot' into the real world and onto the unsuspecting public. The premise is that JK and Joel run the show from *Robostar* HQ, a secret mission-control warehouse kitted out with all kinds of hi-tech gadgetry. From here, the kids control their 'Robostar' through microphones and other kit, and a bank of video screens covering all angles of the action. The kids are central to the show, so in many scenes one of the team will be posted out to where the action is, to take part in the scene. As secret extras, they're also in contact with HQ using hi-tech spy equipment and can affect the action to keep the variety broad. The kids just loved doing the filming and got me to do some seriously embarrassing things.

One of the first challenges I faced was when I had to pretend to want some new photos and the photoshoot would take place at home in my house (not really my house but a set with loads of hidden cameras and microphones). The photographer (someone real on whom the joke was played) was to come to my house and take pictures of me and, via a small in-ear device, the kids would tell me exactly what to say and do to the photographer. I must admit I was a little nervous as I had no clue what the kids would instruct me to do, while the woman photographer would be none the wiser and was likely to think I was completely mad. I was prepped for the scene a few times in another room in the house then the technical team came in to prep my body. I had a tiny hidden camera in my shirt button, which was amazing because there was no way you could tell it was there. Additionally, there were lots of wires taped to my body for sound and vision to capture every moment.

Well … the lady in question arrived and my PA (played by one of the crew) answered the front door and then brought this poor unsuspecting photographer up the stairs to what was my pretend bedroom, where I waited nervously. I was to meet and greet her then launch into the photoshoot. The door opened and it was on, for young and old.

The kids told me secretly to do the photoshoot on the bed but never stop moving positions, as they didn't want her to get a good shot of me. I followed my instructions, of course, as a good Robostar, and, after about twenty different positions on the bed, the photographer was getting hugely frustrated as she couldn't get a good shot. Then the kids changed tack and I had to tell the photographer I now wanted dance photos. But that's not all – I had to dance to their instructions. So they were saying: 'one arm can't stop moving, now your right leg won't stop dancing'; 'dance in the bath'; 'dance around the bath'; 'tell her you have a funny twitch that won't go away'; 'tell her that once you start dancing you just can't stop'.

I couldn't believe the poor photographer was taking it so seriously and it was all I could do not to giggle. The kids then asked me to get the photographer to show me some of her dancing and then I had to get her in the splits! The photographer ended up in the splits; it was amazing to see how gullible people can be. She must have thought me insane and probably couldn't wait to get the money for the shoot and run.

The prank was revealed at this point, thank goodness, before she did herself a mischief of the hamstring variety and, when she found out, she took it in really good part and we all fell about laughing.

The next challenge was to try to get members of the public to join me in the longest conga line around a square in central London. It was such a difficult task, as no one wanted to participate. I had a ghetto-blaster playing music in the middle of the square and a big megaphone to shout out to people to join me. After many failed attempts, I eventually got four people to take part. I don't think they were sound of mind but at least it wasn't a total failure. Highly cringe-worthy, nonetheless – much to the delight of the children.

For the final challenge, I pretended to be holding auditions and invited dancers to a studio to explain my concept for a 'new musical', sitting on a swinging chair placed in the centre of the room. It was to be called *Craig the Musical*. I had to sit the dancers down and tell them that the show was based on my life and give them some choreography to do for the try out. They must have thought me the biggest twat ever!

The children controlling me were telling me what to say and do, and I had to give the dancers a demonstration of the kids' song 'Head, Shoulders, Knees and Toes'. The youngsters auditioning were really good street dancers – trendy, hip-hop, pop and lock types – so this type of choreography was beyond basic, and I was forced to make them do it in a funky street-style way. I then had to ask them to take off their shoes and then had to tell one of the dancers that his feet stank and could he please put his shoes back on. The dancer was so embarrassed and I felt awful. The kids made me say stuff you just wouldn't ever say.

For this last section, we had JK and Joel in the audition, dancing in inappropriate dancewear and donning wigs and headbands. Joel was playing my choreographic dance assistant, demonstrating the dances embarrassingly badly, and I had to say to the pros that that was the way I wanted it and that he was the best dancer I'd ever seen … They then tried to copy his style and that was just farcical. I actually began to laugh during this charade and completely came out of character. Hysterical.

I felt so sorry for the professional dancers and what I put them through and also felt terrible that there was actually no job to be had after all of it. But we relieved them of the ordeal, telling them it was a wind-up and that the whole thing had been filmed, then chatted and relived every moment mirthfully.

# CHAPTER 11
# STRICTLY CONFIDENTIAL

I n the summers of 2012 and 2013, I became a cruise-ship entertainer – of sorts. While many wannabe stars start out on the ships, I went the topsy-turvy route and got on board through my role on *Strictly*.

On the *Strictly Come Dancing* cruises, I travel with two of the show's professionals, such as Natalie Lowe and Ian Waite, Robin and Kristina or Pasha and Katya, and they put on a show for the passengers, and I do a Q&A. Then there are dance classes for the couples on board and a passenger competition, the winners of which get to dance in the *Strictly Come Dancing* Showcase, which I host and judge with the pros.

And I don't pull my punches just because they are paying customers. They would be disappointed if I was too nice to them and they find it funny when I call their routines a 'complete and absolute dance dis-ah-ster'.

The first year, 2012, was a trial year, to test the popularity of such events, and I did two cruises: the first was up through Norway, which was stunning – the scenery was just beautiful – and the second from Las Palmas, Gran Canaria, which sailed back to Southampton. The second year, 2013, I was booked for seven cruises, so have crowbarred those into my already very busy schedule – and there are plans to do even more next year, which is quite frightening. Still, there are a lot worse ways to earn a living.

The ships we travel on are beautiful and, of course, we sail through the most amazing scenery, bringing *Strictly* sparkle to the open seas, on the Med or up around Norway. Ports we visit vary from Gibraltar, Lisbon, Cadiz and the Canary Islands. As a general rule, I'll board the ship during the last three days of the cruise and sail back to Southampton, so I'm always at sea. We always seem to travel through the Bay of Biscay when our shows are on and the swell can be quite big, which means the ship rocks from side to side – making a Rumba virtually impossible to dance – let alone the lifts the professional dancers usually do. One night, Katya and Pasha were doing a *Dirty Dancing* section and it came to the famous lift at the end, where the boy holds the girl directly above his head, as she assumes a bird position, horizontal in the air. The ship rolled just at the crucial moment of Pasha catching and pressing Katya, and they fell out of it. Mortified, they attempted it again and this time the boat behaved and they succeeded.

The previous year there had been another incident when Ian and Natalie were doing a foxtrot together and Natalie stepped backwards and fell off the stage, only to be caught by an unsuspecting passenger who was innocently sitting in the front row. The passengers talked about that for the rest of the cruise.

I really enjoy getting a chance to mix with all these devoted fans of the show, who have paid money to, number one, have a fab-u-lous holiday and, secondly, be on the same ship as us, and I love popping into the dance classes to give them a bit of encouragement. It's brilliant to see all those couples having a go at dancing and we have a right giggle as they do their first cha-cha-cha, or attempt a waltz.

On one cruise, I bumped into Richard Dunwoody, who had competed in series seven of *Strictly*, with Lilia Kopylova. He hadn't been the best dancer, sadly, and had exited early, just behind the first casualty, tennis player Martina Hingis.

I learned he was on the ship and I surprised him by going to see his Q&A session and that was quite funny because we had a bit of a banter and a bit of joke about how dreadful he was on the dance floor. He clearly had no delusions of grandeur about being a fabulous dancer, but he had a great time and he spoke very fondly about *Strictly*, which was good to hear.

My Q&A audiences are packed to the rafters and they are a great way of communicating to the fans and being myself. They learn a lot about me and can ask me anything – and I mean anything – and will always get a straight and honest answer. It's great because they can see the real me and not just the Mr Nasty they see on the telly. I talk a little about my life and how and why I started dancing and also how I got the *Strictly* gig. It's a lot of fun and interesting for me as well.

The first thing people on board always say is, 'My goodness, you're tall!' Then the next thing is, 'You look so much younger than on the telly!' And, 'You're so much slimmer in real life' is another. Well, it's often said that telly puts ten pounds and ten years on you – and there's the proof! The reason they are surprised by my height is that on *Strictly*, I'm always sitting at a desk and you can't see my legs. The judges are all matched so that our eye-lines are on a level with one another, which is achieved by the clever placement of cushions on seats for Darcey and Bruno, who are both shorter than Len and I.

After my Q&A, many people tell me that I'm much nicer in real life, but that's because when I'm just chatting to them I'm not judging. While on board, I also have a two-hour photo session with the passengers, followed by a book signing. It's all very pleasant and a wonderful opportunity to speak to the people, and they get a chance to have their say about the programme, whether it be complaints or praise. It's good to know what the fans think and have their opinion, because it counts. God knows, I have opinions about everything and have become famous for them, so I say, 'Bring it on!'

On every cruise, we all meet the captain and some of the crew, get taken up to the bridge, which is amazing, and have dinner with the captain. We also socialize with the resident dancers from the Headliner Company and other entertainers on board. The *Strictly* cruises are a resounding success because our audience can get up-close and personal with us. Everyone on board is encouraged to dance and enter the passenger competition. Some are reluctant (and I'm not surprised as they will ultimately be judged by me!), but everything I say there is tongue in cheek, as I wouldn't want to spoil anyone's holiday by ripping them to shreds on their last couple of days. All in all, it's a delightful and inspiring way to bring *Strictly* to the audience.

Like our *Strictly* Come Dancing Live tour, the pro tour, where our amazing professional couples show off all their dances, was proving a huge success with the public. Thinking about both shows, it planted in me the seed of an idea and I thought, 'I wonder if it would be possible to do something that isn't all demonstration dancing. Something a bit more personal?' The dancing is excellent and wonderful to watch, but you don't really get to know the dancers at all, so I began to picture a show that wasn't just dance after dance, but that informed the dance choices with something personal from the lives of the performers.

I began thinking of the musical *A Chorus Line*, which introduces you to the dancers and reveals what makes them want to dance, what makes them tick. This makes the dance more watchable because they're doing it for a reason, and they are generally personal reasons. The professionals on our show never really get the chance to speak about themselves and their lives, and they've become celebrities in their own right and I thought it would be really interesting to mix a combination of pro dancers with one of the show's celebs, as an ensemble. That's how I came up with my touring show, *Strictly Confidential*.

Once I'd come up with the concept I had to find the right celebrity to star in it. I was looking for someone who could head this, so ideally an actor or an actress; it needed to be someone who can dance a bit, someone enthusiastic, likeable and, if possible, someone who can sing a bit as well, because we wanted to mix up the genre a little. *Strictly* has become so very theatrical now, with a lot of the stories woven into it, so I thought the show could just take the *Strictly* pro tour and make it more informative, drawing the audience more into the real lives of the dancers.

Previously, I'd had Anita Dobson in mind, because she's a good all-rounder and a good character. Then I thought Denise Van Outen could do it, or Jill Halfpenny, anyone who can do the song-and-dance routines as well as act. Kara Tointon was in the frame when I wrote a treatment of the show to pitch to the BBC and to Phil McIntyre and Stage Entertainment. That version involved Kara Tointon and Artem's story because I thought that would interest *Strictly* fans and I wanted Kristina and Robin as well, because the four of them are close friends and have interesting stories to tell ...

However, Kara and Artem did another *Strictly* production called *Dance to the Music* and then Kara wanted to go back onto the stage as an actor. Robin and Kristina went into *Burn the Floor* and so were unavailable. But there were a lot of people to choose from ... Anton and Erin Malloy would be great but they do their own show ... Vincent and Flavia would be great, but they do their own show ... you just need people who have strong personalities.

Then I decided Ian Waite could do it because people love him and we hadn't seen much of him on the screens – apart from on *It Takes Two*. It would be nice to find out a little bit about him, how he felt about leaving *Strictly*, as a competing professional. And Natalie Lowe, who's still part of *Strictly*, and who dances with Ian.

The glamorous Natalie Lowe, who also stars in my show, *Strictly Confidential*.

Just as we were wondering which celebrity fitted the bill, along came Lisa Riley. Lisa's story was heartbreaking as well as uplifting, and she's had a fantastic career to date, so I wrote her an autobiographical script to which she reacted really well. We talked about it on tour and she was really keen to do it, so it was all systems go.

As I didn't have Robin, Lisa's pro partner from the series, due to his commitments with his West End show, I decided to get his best friend, Artem Chigvintsev, on board to dance with Lisa. This turned out to be a spectacular partnership and he has a very interesting past, having grown up in Russia, then moved to the States and come to a final stop in the UK. His body wasn't bad either, and that, I knew, would be a draw in itself!

So, there was my line-up: Lisa as the headliner then her co-stars Artem, Natalie and Ian. I also needed an ensemble of four commercial dancers and five multi-talented singer/dancer/actor/musicians to provide the music and singing.

Now I needed to dig up some dirt on our stars, so conducted a series of recorded interviews with each of them about their hopes, dreams, passions, loves, hates and why they began to dance. From their stories, I chose the music, and finally put the whole show together.

I employed the amazing services of choreographer, Jason Gilkison – now Head of Choreography on *Strictly*

*Come Dancing* – to provide spectacular dance routines, and the incredible Sarah Travis, Tony Award-winner for best arrangements for *Sweeney Todd*, with whom I've worked for years in the theatre trade, to come up with fantastic arrangements for the music. Lighting had to be amazing, so I got my good friend and colleague Richard G. Jones to make it look beautiful, and set designer Morgan Large to give us a platform on which to set the show. As you can see, the director is responsible for putting the team in place in order to create one vision for the piece. It was a joy to work on and the cast were all so excited to be doing something different and new.

Our world premiere was in Plymouth at The Pavilions – a matinée and an evening show – and the crowds went wild! Both shows had standing ovations and that trend continued in every venue we toured. It even got the Southend-on-Sea Cliffs Pavilion rumble, which is where everyone in the audience stamps their feet to create an explosive deep rumbling sound that feels like it will bring the theatre crashing down to the ground!

I'm really pleased for Lisa that the show went well and that she was able to show the UK what she can do. She really was the star of the show.

# CHAPTER 12

# LIFE IS JUST A BOWL OF CHERRIES

In the summer of 2012, I was approached to direct and choreograph *Fiddler on the Roof*. I was very excited by the prospect of staging this show with actor/musos, as it lends itself to a Gypsy-style band and written into the show is an onstage band for the wedding scene and various other musical moments. I was also able to employ a company of more than my normal twelve, which made the whole idea appealing. I soon went to work to do the casting and, naturally, the role of Tevye, played by Topol in the film, was my biggest concern. It had to be someone special who could also put bums on seats and deliver. We went through a list of various names and then the brilliant idea of asking Paul Michael Glaser cropped up. Paul is most famous for playing the role of Starsky in *Starsky and Hutch,* opposite David Soul, but he also played the role of Perchik in the 1971 film of *Fiddler,* so I thought this would be an amazing theatrical coup.

The film, directed by Norman Jewison, was an adaption of the 1964 Broadway musical, with music by Jerry Bock, lyrics by Sheldon Harnick and the screenplay by Joseph Stein. It did very well, winning three Academy Awards, including one for the arranger-conductor John Williams. It was also nominated for several more, including Best Picture, Best Actor for Topol and Best Supporting Actor for Leonard Frey, who played the part of Motel Kamzoil. Topol, of course, played it in the original London stage production and, for our show, having an actor on board like Paul Michael Glaser (PMG), who had worked alongside Topol, was so very exciting. The fact that he's now exactly the right age to play Tevye just made it doubly exciting.

To our delight, when we approached PMG to do it, he was beside himself with excitement, as he's an actor who simply loves the stage. Add that to the chance to play the lead in the show after creating Perchik, a radical Marxist from Kiev, for the film, and it was his dream come true.

A phone call was arranged, in which I would speak to him about my thoughts on the project, concept, design, how I see the character etc., and the most bizarre situation followed. When the phone went I was a tiny bit nervous and excited all at once, I must admit, as I grew up with *Starsky and Hutch* in Australia: I watched it religiously; I was a real fan. I answered the call and introduced myself, then waited for a reply – which soon came in those unmistakably distinctive tones. I thought to myself, 'Oh, my God, it's Starsky! I'm *actually* speaking to Starsky!' His voice had not changed and, to be truthful, I was a little bit star-struck.

The usual pleasantries followed, then we began speaking about the show but I could hear all this background noise, so asked him where he was. He said he was in his car, driving to a studio to do some filming in LA. It sounded so starry – and I was loving it! So, he's there in his car, driving along, then he suddenly launches into a Tevye monologue and starts to sing 'If I Were a Rich Man' down the telephone.

That was his audition! It's the oddest audition I think I've ever done – apart from the one I did around a pool when I was in Broome in North Western Australia on a holiday and had to cast the leading lady for a show called *Spend Spend Spend* on my computer via a satellite link. The actress, Karen Mann, went on to win the Theatrical Management Association (TMA) Award for Best Actress in a Musical for the role of Viv Nicholson, so it couldn't have been all that bad.

Anyway, my childhood hero, PMG, was great on the telephone and landed the job. Then it was time to meet him in the flesh.

We met on the first day of rehearsals, on a Monday. I'd just been up to Leeds to see the final two shows of *Strictly Confidential* the day before, and I travelled back to London on the company tour bus with the cast, which, inevitably, ended up being a mad party bus with everyone reminiscing about the show and how sad it was to finish the tour. It was a night where everyone could let their hair down and relax. The bus didn't leave until about 11:30 p.m., so we didn't get back to our homes until four in the morning, frankly all a bit worse for wear. I had a couple of hours' sleep then had to go to our first day of rehearsals for *Fiddler* that very morning, at nine.

I always start with the meet-and-greet, which involves the entire company standing in a very large circle in the rehearsal space and introducing themselves one by one, including producers, stage management, publicity, people from the office, sound, lighting, design, wardrobe and, of course, the actors. It starts with me doing my welcome speech and then we go around the room anti-clockwise. Some people get very nervous as it's the first day and you don't know everyone. They have to say their names and what they are doing with the show or in the show. It's always quite funny because some people stumble, some speak loudly, some crack one-liners and try to be funny, some ensemble members have no clue what parts they will be playing and simply say, 'My name is … and I'm chorus.' Some even said their name and then, 'I think I'm playing a Jew?' The circle always gets a laugh and breaks the ice.

It finally got to PMG, who had situated himself halfway around the circle, and he went into a great big speech about how excited he was to be here etc., which was lovely. All the rest of the company's speeches had been quite short till then, simply stating their name and job. At the end of PMG's speech, I piped up and thanked him, then went on to explain to the company that this particular production was an ensemble piece, there are no stars, we all work together as a team to create something truly fantastic that we can all be proud of, although some of us *do* have our names above the title (PMG) and some of us *do* have our names on the poster in a box (me). Then I went on to say, 'Of course, that was a major bone of contention but naturally it's all settled now.' I wasn't intending any malice and was just breaking the ice for the company.

You see, it was a bit of an 'in' joke with PMG's and my management as my name was originally above the title as

'Craig Revel Horwood's *Fiddler on the Roof* but that was changed to 'PMG starring in ...' and my name ended up in a box below the title. It matters not. I find all of that stuff amusing – as people at home probably never even consider it – but I've been through many of these situations, where it is contractual and stipulated by the artist, for instance, where and how big their name will appear on the poster – even down to the type of font that's used! It's a funny old business, this one they call 'show', but it is serious too and can also be a deal-breaker. In past shows, I've heard various artists bitching in corridors about how someone's name is bigger than theirs on the poster. Once, for the *Spend Spend Spend* opening night in the West End, my name in the programme had a typing error, so instead of Craig Revel Horwood it read Craig Revel Howrood! Ha ha! How rude indeed. That was so funny and I've laughed about it for years but, to add insult to injury, the CV of the designer, Les Brotherston, was under my misspelt name. It read, 'Les began his career ... ' The entire company were in hysterics backstage. I don't expect most people read them anyway and you can't take it too seriously. I certainly didn't.

PMG was equally unfazed by these things, and we had a chuckle about it all and get on really well. He is a delight and a pleasure to work with, as are the whole company. I'm just in awe of talent and at times like these I just love my job. I'm so very lucky and honoured to work with the most incredible people and never ever take one minute for granted.

It was thirteen years ago that *The Witches of Eastwick* – a 2000 musical based on the novel of the same name by John Updike – first opened at the Theatre Royal, Drury Lane. The story is based around three women, the 'Witches' – Alexandra Spofford, Jane Smart and Sukie Rougemont – who are bored by their small-town existence in Eastwick. When a charismatic and decadent stranger, Darryl Van Horne, comes to town, each of the three women is seduced in turn and their inner powers are unlocked. Their hedonistic lifestyle causes scandal in the quiet town and events take a sinister turn when they wish evil on a female enemy, with disastrous results. As the women come to realize that Darryl's influence is corrupting everyone, they turn their new-found powers on him, in a bid to get rid of him.

I have quite a history with this particular piece, as I mentioned at length in my last book, *All Balls and Glitter*. To summarize, shortly after I had put on *Spend Spend Spend* in the West End, Cameron Mackintosh phoned to tell me about *The Witches of Eastwick*. It was an exciting project and I was led to believe I would be doing it alone, but American choreographer Bob Avian was brought on board after the audition period and instead of the title of co-choreographer, I was offered the lesser title of associate choreographer, which would mean I had no rights to the choreography and would be working under someone else's name again.

After raising my complaint with Cameron, he told me, 'You don't understand comedy.'

'I have just choreographed *Spend Spend Spend*,' I replied. 'That is a comedy, Cameron, and I was nominated for an Olivier Award for it!'

'Yes, dear, *that* is a British comedy,' he said, snippily. '*Witches* is an American comedy.'

Humiliated and upset, I quit the job. A month later, I was called back to Cameron's company, CamMac, for a meeting. I assumed he wanted to beg me to return, so I was happy to go along and talk. No such luck. After keeping me waiting for an hour, he told me he had called me in to tell me the job had now gone to a friend and colleague of mine, Stephen Mears – who would be billed as co-choreographer, the very title I had asked for!

That was a slap in the face because I had been working to make my name in the theatre and *Spend* had been a big breakthrough. I wanted to keep up the momentum and be recognized as the creative force behind the shows. But that setback, as I said in *All Balls and Glitter*, put me in the poor house for ages.

The Watermill Theatre is another labour of love that puts you in the poor house. It's partly Arts Council funded and is a registered charity but it's a place where I can be free to create.

The small but thriving theatre creates great shows that audiences love. From its home in a beautiful converted Watermill in rural Berkshire, it produces award-winning work that has been recognized throughout the UK and abroad. It also enjoys West End transfers and national and international tours and gives directors and creative teams the space to develop new work, so it's a leading force in cultivating the theatre-makers of tomorrow. The ethos at the Watermill is based on a sense of community, with acting companies, stage management and creative teams living and working on site. This environment demands a commitment to the work that encourages a true sense of ensemble that is visible on stage. The space is extremely intimate, a 220-seat auditorium, which also means that there is a remarkably strong connection between the actors and the audience, making this theatre a very special place. It has a thriving education-and-participation programme, which works with around 16,000 people every year and relies on ongoing support from donors that enables them to fully deliver an artistic programme. Without it they would struggle to survive.

Support is crucial to the theatre and that's why I love working there. By the way, they still need donations! As a registered charity, the Watermill Theatre aims to break even each financial year. Approximately eighty-five per cent of their revenue income is generated by their own activities – box-office sales, restaurant sales, sponsorship, donations and merchandise. The remaining fifteen per cent is received from the Arts Council of England SE and West Berkshire Council and investments.

I have been working at the Watermill for many years and shows have included *The Hot Mikado*, *Martin Guerre*, *Spend Spend Spend*, *Copacabana* and, most recently, *The Witches of Eastwick*. Yes, it came back to me in a delightful full circle. Thirteen years on, I was finally getting the chance to not only choreograph it but direct it as well.

The opportunity only came up because the Watermill had lost the director of the 2013 summer season, as she was having a baby; so Hedda Beeby, the director of the charity, phoned and asked if I was available. I wasn't actually completely available due to the fact I was doing the *Strictly* cruises intermittently over the whole summer but I said I would mull it over ... and then there was deciding what show to do. Hedda mentioned *Witches* and I thought, 'Ooh, that would be a good one.' It got my attention straight away, not only because it's a great show but also because I'd be able to show Cameron what I could do with the piece and what he missed out on thirteen years previously. However, there was also the small matter of getting the rights from him first, and I would have to have several meetings with him to persuade him to license the show to us. I would have to prove that it would be in his interests as well as in the Watermill's – and mine.

After several conversations, Cameron agreed and I managed to crowbar the rehearsals around all my other commitments. The dates all worked out, I employed an assistant, the adorable David Hulston, who has been helping me out for several years, and he was to be on hand to keep the rehearsals going on my absent days, while I was performing on the ships. I normally do the Watermill shows by myself, without an assistant, but it was so essential for the show to work that David's talents came to good use, as I only had sixteen rehearsal days to get the show up and running. I was away for four days twice during the rehearsal time so it had to run like clockwork – and it did!

I was literally scheduled to within an inch of my life, what with writing this book, the cruises, pre-production on

*Witches* and casting for my next project, *Fiddler on the Roof*, plus my commitment to *Strictly Confidential*. It was all a bit chaotic to say the least. I didn't have a day off for two months and every lunch hour was taken up with the many interviews to publicize all three shows. Yes, it was busy, but I had put together an extremely talented team who could deliver the show I dreamed of.

The rehearsals were fun and I had employed one of the best casts ever. Alex Bourne, our leading man, was just perfect for the role of the demonic Darryl van Horne. The three witches, Poppy Tierney, Tiffany Graves and Joanne Hickman, were a complete sensation. The support cast was incredible too and I had been able to acquire the services of the original creator of the part of Felicia Gabriel from the Theatre Royal, Drury Lane, production back in 2000, the amazing actress and singer, Rosie Ashe. She was hilarious to work with.

During the show, Rosie had to produce – or vomit – various outrageous items from her mouth. The witches cast a spell on her and place various objects into their 'cauldron' (that was actually represented by a cookie jar) and she, in turn, heaves them up and pulls them out of her mouth. This requires an enormous amount of skill, so we decided to get a magician in for the rehearsals to teach her how to do it. The list was hilarious: a tennis ball, a dead Egret, a string of pearls, a golf ball, loads of coins and feathers, but the *pièce de résistance* was projectile vomiting cherry pits onto a wall.

Our production supervisor Laurence came up with a great idea for this particular scene by using a soda fountain. It was genius! The fountain was placed in a vase full of flowers on a table so the audience couldn't see it, and filled with this red slimy gunk. All Rosie had to do was then place her mouth to the vase as if she was going to be sick in it and pull down the lever to release the 'vomit' onto the back wall of the home bar on the set. It was an amazing effect and had the capacity to go on for about five minutes! It's not very high tech but extremely effective and it brought the house down every time.

After that, Rosie vomits a never-ending ream of paper, which her husband Clyde uses to strangle her to death. Clyde was played by the wonderful Jeffrey Harmer, with whom I've previously worked in *The Hot Mikado*, in which he gave us his sublime portrayal of the character Ko-Ko. Rosie and Jeffrey hit it off from the beginning and the room was constantly full of laughter. Rosie has never really been much of a mover – and by that I mean dancing doesn't come naturally to her, although she works tirelessly at it and gets there in the end; but she does get herself into a muddle on occasion. In one rehearsal, we were going through a number in the show called 'Dirty Laundry'.

I set the stage up with three washing lines; one upstage, one mid-stage and one downstage. The characters gossip away while placing various bits of laundry on the line and, as it's a musical number, everything has to be timed to perfection.

Rosie was required to make her entrance behind a big white sheet and miraculously, after the unfolding of the sheet, be discovered, centre stage, for her song. On this occasion, the timing went somewhat awry and, as she entered the space she misjudged her walk forward and ended up with the big white sheet completely over her head for her song. The creative team and cast fell about laughing but she soldiered on with the number. Her fellow actors managed to get the sheet back off her head, dragging her downstage with the force of their tugging, then the whole company launched into a very fast dance break, involving kick lines and very quick swapping of upstage and downstage washing lines. Rosie got into a terrible muddle with the entire sequence, which involves her spinning a few times beneath the washing lines, and she ended up with one line being caught around her wrist, cutting off the blood supply to her left hand, and another double wrapped around her neck strangling her – a little earlier than such a fate was due. At this point, I felt there was nothing to be done except to place a stop to the proceedings and say, 'Shall we try that again from the top?'

That is just one of Rosie's many misfortunes in the dance department but it always made for a good laugh and kept us amused throughout the entire rehearsal period.

The three witches open act two with a song entitled 'Another Night at Darryl's', during which they end up in a mud wrestling fight. One of the witches, Jo, has to pour the remainder of the bucket of mud over the other two girls as they wrestle on a sheet of plastic on the stage. During one of the performances, the stage management had set the wrong consistency for the mud and it was a little runnier than normal. It was too late to do much about it so we ploughed on with the scene anyway. Well, the Watermill Theatre is a very small venue and the audience is very close to the stage. As the girls performed this mucky scene, on this occasion, the mud went everywhere – bouncing of the walls, going all over the set, the instruments and covering the entire front row in mud. The screaming that ensued was a joy. The Watermill's dry-cleaning bill, however, was not!

The show opened to great reviews and was a huge box-office success. I couldn't have been more chuffed when all that hard worked finally paid off. It was great to show Cameron Mackintosh what I could do with it – and that's why I love the Watermill.

Although I have got used to being single, it does provide some challenges for me. Dating for me is not simple and, while other people can join dating websites, I have to be careful what I put out there.

I have had my fair share of dating disasters. One guy I met, who sounded great on paper, turned out to be dull, dull, dull. I took him out to the theatre, because I thought that was a good place to meet, and we went with friends, so I thought that would take the pressure off, we could all get together and see how it goes. But it was a really dreadful evening.

Then there was a guy from Wales, who was gorgeous, we got on really well and everything was brilliant in the bedroom, but, somehow, I didn't think he was completely right. He was thirty-three and a bit too young.

One ex-boyfriend from years ago – known as 'Little Big Dick' because he was short with quite a substantial piece of equipment – came back around after I split with Grant and wanted to get back together and I didn't know what to do about that, because I was so worried that I'd be leading him up the garden path if I rekindled the romance and wasn't able to fulfil the relationship that he wanted. He wanted an everlasting long-term relationship but I don't think it would have worked. You have to acquire a relationship first to even consider it, and even then, when that comes along and you think this is perfect, it never is. So since Grant, with the exception of Doctor D, it's been fumbles in the dark.

The funny thing is, I'm still looking for Mr Right. He may not exist but I do live in hope that one day again I'll love and be loved in return. It sounds simple, doesn't it? Get the violins out, darling, and let's make music!

Life is improvised and you have to make the most of it. As Shakespeare quite rightly put it:

*All the world's a stage,*
*And all the men and women merely players,*
*They have their exits and their entrances,*
*And one man in his time plays many parts.*

And I have and will continue to do so.

# ACKNOWLEDGEMENTS

Let me begin by saying how wonderful it was to pen *Tales from the Dance Floor* and to have been given another opportunity by my publishers, Michael O'Mara Books, to do so. They were a pleasure to work with on the book and all the staff there are so talented and friendly. A special mention and thank you must go to Senior Editorial Director, Louise Dixon, and Alison Parker, Deputy Managing Director for continually pushing me to be better, the constant supply of deadlines, which I desperately needed, and making great editorial choices.

Thanks to one of my great friends and colleagues, Alison Maloney, for the endless interviews and transcripts she provided and for making sense of all of my ramblings. Ali also came up with fab-u-lous ideas for the book, for which I can't thank her enough.

My family, all of whom, once again, have gone out on yet another limb, putting up with my honesty and portrayal of family life. I love them all very much and without their support I would not be who I am today.

Grant, for being one of the most supportive ex-boyfriends who is now one of my very closest friends and whom I will always love unconditionally.

To all the dearly departed close friends I have lost and mentioned in the book, as they shaped the person I am today and will be in the future.

The love and support of my work colleagues, who have got me through the good and bad times, filled my life with laughs and provided me with sanity through the most stressful moments of my life.

My gorgeous PA of four years, Clare Fox, without whom I never would be able to achieve anything. Clare is a solid rock in my life and organizes my diary to within an inch of its life, supporting not only my career but my personal life too. I couldn't do it all without you, Clare, and bow down to your talents and skills.

My manager and friend, Gavin Barker, and his incredible team at Gavin Barker Associates have been an amazing support. Gavin is a master at helping me make decisions on a professional level and, not only that, is someone I can go to whenever there may be doubt or demons in my life.

Thanks to the BBC and *Strictly Come Dancing* for giving me endless opportunities and a platform on which to speak, and providing me with the best Saturday job in the world, for which I'll forever be indebted. It's such a great place to work and really provides a close *Strictly* family atmosphere. They really do care about the people who work for them and that means so very much.

Last but by no means least, the *Strictly Come Dancing* fans for their continued support and without whom there would be no *Strictly*. Where would classy, clean, family-friendly Saturday-night entertainment be without *Strictly*?

Finally, thank you for purchasing the book; I hope you enjoyed reading it as much as I have had the great pleasure of writing it.

Craig Revel Horwood

# INDEX